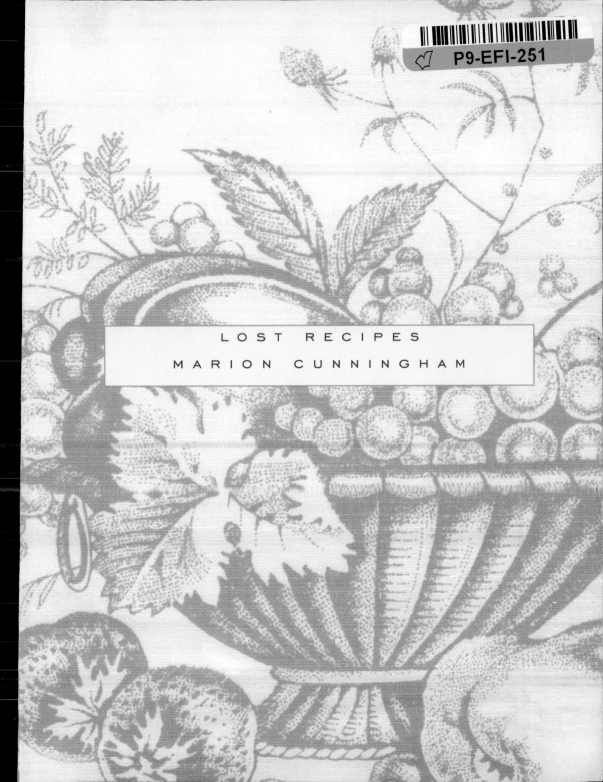

LOST   RECIPES

MARION   CUNNINGHAM

LOST RECIPES

MARION CUNNINGHAM

ALSO BY MARION CUNNINGHAM

Learning to Cook with Marion Cunningham

Cooking with Children

The Supper Book

The Breakfast Book

The Fannie Farmer Baking Book

The Fannie Farmer Cookbook

DISH

LOST RECIPES

STYLECRAFT, BALTO. 30, MD.   PRINTED IN U.S.A.

USA 20

Our

ʼn

com

LOST RECIPES

MEALS TO SHARE WITH FRIENDS AND FAMILY

MARION CUNNINGHAM

COLLAGE ILLUSTRATIONS BY CAROL DEVINE CARSON

ALFRED A. KNOPF NEW YORK 2005

Grateful acknowledgment is made to the following for permission
to reprint previously published material:
Alfred A. Knopf and Jeffrey Steingarten: Excerpt from *The Man Who Ate Everything* by
Jeffrey Steingarten. Copyright © 1997 by Jeffrey Steingarten. Reprinted by permission
of Alfred A. Knopf, a division of Random House Inc. and the author.
The Guardian: Excerpts from "Fat Is the Outward and Visible Sign of Social Disaster" by
Felipe Fernandez-Armesto from *The Guardian* (September 9, 2002). Copyright © 2002
by Felipe Fernandez-Armesto. Reprinted by permission of *The Guardian.*
New York Times: Excerpts from "Cooking, and How It Slew the Beast . . ." by Natalie
Angier from the *New York Times* (May 28, 2002). Copyright © 2002 by the New York
Times Co. Reprinted by permission of the *New York Times.*
People Magazine: Excerpts from an article by Dr. Richard Strauss from *People Weekly*
(February 19, 2001). Copyright © 2001 by Time Inc. All rights reserved. Reprinted by
permission of *People Magazine.*
U.S. News & World Report: Excerpt from "Keeping the Flame Alive" from *U.S. News &
World Report* (August 16, 1999). Copyright © 1999 by U.S. News & World Report, L.P.
Reprinted by permission of the *U.S. News & World Report.*

Library of Congress Cataloging-in-Publication Data
Cunningham, Marion.
Lost recipes / by Marion Cunningham.
p.   cm.
Includes index.
ISBN 0-375-41198-4
1. Cookery, American. I. Title.
TX715.C96274 2003
641.5973—dc21   2002043323

Manufactured in Malaysia
Published October 22, 2003
Second Printing, September 2005

CONTENTS

ACKNOWLEDGMENTS

First and foremost, I want to thank Judith Jones for the great opportunity of working with her and of learning from her the very basics of how to write a cookbook. Her knowledge and patience are impressive. James Beard and Judith Jones opened a door that has given me a wonderful life and many, many rewards for thirty years.

My appreciation also for the effort and assistance that was given by my daughter, Catherine Cunningham; my friends and helpers Amanda Haas, Josie Norton, Carol Fowler; and my friend of many years, Betsy Feichtmeir. Last, but certainly not least, Ken Schneider has been a great help making corrections and putting them on the disk—and his wonderful sense of humor can lift one out of the doldrums instantly.

INTRODUCTION

Recently I read the results of two different surveys on home cooking—one reporting that about 40 percent of the population cooks at home, the other that only 30 percent does. No matter the exact percentages, one thing we know for sure is that fewer and fewer people are cooking, either because they don't know how or because they just don't want to bother.

I think this is a greater loss than we realize. Home cooking is a catalyst that brings people together. We are losing the daily ritual of sitting down around the table (without the intrusion of television), of having the opportunity to interact, to share our experiences and concerns, to listen to others. Home kitchens, despite the increase in designer appliances and cabinetry, are mostly quiet and empty today. Strangers are preparing much of our food. And our supermarkets, which once considered restaurants and fast-food places the enemy, have joined the trend by enlarging their delis and offering ready-to-eat food they call "home-replacement meals." But bringing ready-cooked meals home is not the same as cooking something in your own kitchen, where you are in control of the ingredients you use, where you fill the house with good cooking smells, and where you all share in a single dish, taking a helping and passing the platter on to your neighbor. Nothing can replace that.

Why are fewer people cooking at home? There are, of course, a multitude of reasons—with pressures of time and of conflicting schedules, football practice and PTA meetings, all usurping the dinner hour. But there is one reason that is paramount, I think: Home cooking in America has long been considered menial drudgery.

This sentiment is not hard to understand. Struggling immigrants did not want to see their children in this land of golden opportunity spending their lives slaving away in the kitchens of others. They had bigger dreams. Neither did many women, denied opportunities in other areas, want their daughters to be defined by housework.

It was easy, then, for big commercial food companies to sell their goods with the promise that their boxes, cans, and bags of food could be ready to eat in minutes. Later, microwave ovens promised even quicker results, with little or no cleanup necessary.

There's been almost no counterargument. We home cooks have never gathered in force to speak out in defense of home cooking. So the image of cookery as drudgery lives on.

However, I know firsthand that in addition to being much healthier and more economical than convenience and take-out food, home cooking can be rewarding. For most of my life, I raised a family and my favorite pastime was baking. I baked so many cupcakes for the PTA over the years that if I had sold them instead, I could have retired some time ago a millionaire. And I still love to bake cookies or to have friends in for a Sunday brunch of waffles or a hearty winter supper of soup.

Another of the special pleasures the home cook enjoys is exchanging recipes. I always enjoy it when someone gives me a recipe that he or she is passionate about; it is a real connection with that person. There is something communal about having shared recipes, about passing tastes and flavors from friend to friend and from generation to generation. A fine Southern writer, Bill Neal, wrote in his book *Biscuits, Spoonbread, and Sweet Potato Pie:* "Our food tells us where we came from and who we have become."

It is particularly rewarding to shop at farmers' markets. Instead of pushing carts through endless supermarket aisles, in farmers' markets we stroll from stall to stall, talking with one another, and the subject is invariably the wonderful fresh produce and how to make the most of it.

Home cooking is very different from what the pros do in restaurant kitchens. I think that in recent years too many cookbooks and magazines have emphasized the chef-inspired spectacular dish that takes a long time to prepare and requires too many hard-to-get ingredients. A lot of young people have told me that cooking at home is too expensive because much of what they buy for some special recipe just goes to waste.

But they are misguided. And that's because they don't realize what home cooking really is. It is not concentrating on one special dish at a time that is meant to impress your guests. Instead, we home cooks usually shop just once or twice a week, so we have to plan ahead. If we have a roast on Sunday, it will do for several meals, maybe just cold with some relishes one night when everyone has a heavy schedule, and re-incarnated as hash another night; if we're cooking chicken, we might roast a second one or cook some extra parts so that we can make that lovely rice dish Country Captain *(page 122)* or Chicken Pie *(page 126)* or Chicken, Fruit, and Curry Salad *(page 147)*.

Home cooks also like recipes that can be done ahead so that if friends are coming over or if football practice runs late, a stew or a gratin of vegetables that is already cooked can simply be reheated.

In many ways, home cooking is even more creative than what chefs do, because we improvise rather than do the same dish over and over. It's a challenge to look into the refrigerator and think, What shall I do with this bit of meat or leftover polenta? We also have the fun of cooking together with our children or with friends. And there is a satisfaction in giving pleasure and comfort to others with something we have cooked ourselves.

So this book is addressed to all of you who are tempted to give home cooking a second chance. The recipes I have gathered here were lost primarily because people were no longer cooking in that same kind of home rhythm. But I hope to lure you back into the kitchen with them. Maybe these dishes will bring back the past, providing for some of you a little nostalgia and for others an introduction to good, clean, pure flavors that you never get in take-out food.

LOST RECIPES

SOUPS— THE POT THAT NEEDS NO WATCHING

Emergency Soup

Gazpacho

Vichyssoise

Cold Cucumber Soup
    with Mint

Corn Chowder

Cioppino

Seafood Stew

Cream of Tomato Soup

Mulligatawny Soup

Chicken and
    Dumpling Soup

Ham and Bean Soup

Anytime Split Pea Soup

Tomato Bread Soup

Cream of Celery Soup

Simple Summer
    Vegetable Soup

Simple Winter
    Vegetable Soup

Turkey Soup

Mustard
    Green Soup

Oatmeal Soup

In the old days, every kitchen had a soup pot simmering on the back of the stove. That's no longer practical, but we do have refrigerators and freezers to store a bit of cooked rice or pasta, meat scraps, and vegetable trimmings, all of which add flavor and texture to any soup.

So use recipes such as my Emergency Soup, Simple Summer and Simple Winter Vegetable Soups, Turkey Soup, and Mustard Green Soup as guidelines, improvising with what you have on hand. Many of the heartier soups here, such as Cioppino, Seafood Stew, Mulligatawny, and Ham and Bean Soup, can be your main dish for supper or lunch.

EMERGENCY SOUP

—◌ As a home cook, there are certain lessons that one learns over the years. The one lesson that I learned late was the importance of having a few recipes that could be made quickly if unexpected guests dropped in, or even a neighbor who was lonesome and just needed to share a simple supper to feel better. These recipes are "emergency recipes," and I keep a file of them, ready at all times for the spontaneous meal. They call for ingredients that you need to always have on hand. Emergency Soup is a fine example of what I mean. I serve it with a green salad and warm crackers.

4 cups chicken broth
1 carrot, chopped
1 rib celery, chopped
1 medium onion, chopped
1 cup small shell pasta
Salt and black pepper to taste
1 cup grated Parmesan cheese

Put the broth in a pot and bring to a boil. Add the carrot, celery, and onion and boil gently for 10 minutes, then add the pasta and simmer for 5 minutes. Bite into a pasta shell; when it is tender, the soup is done. Correct the seasoning, adding salt and pepper as needed. A lot depends on how highly seasoned your broth is; some canned chicken broths tend to be quite salty.

Serve in bowls and sprinkle with some grated Parmesan cheese.

NOTE: In summer you might replace the carrot, celery, and onion with 2 unpeeled zucchini grated directly into the broth, then cooked with pasta only 5 minutes. ◌—

ABOUT CHICKEN BROTH

A lot of recipes call for a certain amount of chicken broth in either soups or sauces. Today we get excellent canned chicken broths, so there's no need to make your own. But if you do want to and have extra chicken parts such as backbones, necks (if you can get them), and gizzards (not livers), it is very simple to make a flavorful broth. I find that if you get in the habit of cutting up the whole chicken yourself to use the breast, legs, thighs, and wings in a recipe, pretty soon you will collect these leftover parts in your freezer and have enough to make broth.

TO MAKE THE BROTH: Just simmer about 2 cups of raw chicken pieces in 2 quarts of water, with a medium onion, a few cut-up carrots, and parsley stems or celery leaves if you have them; season with a little salt and pepper (not too much because the broth cooks down and the flavors intensify). Cook gently for about 1½ hours, then strain off the broth. And there you have it—about 6 cups of chicken broth to store and use as you wish. And it cost you almost nothing. It will keep refrigerated up to a week and can be frozen for a couple of months.

A lot of people use leftover cooked chicken bones to make broth, but I find that the final flavor of the soup lacks character and depth. Because of this, I would recommend using the cooked carcass and adding at least some raw chicken parts to liven up the soup. You can even buy a small package of wings for that purpose.

GAZPACHO

—↷ This Spanish soup is as lively and appealing as a mariachi. Lovely on a hot summer day.

2 cucumbers, peeled, seeded, and coarsely chopped *(see Note)*
5 tomatoes, peeled and chopped (about 2½ cups)
1 large onion, chopped
1 green bell pepper, seeded, ribbed, and chopped *(see Note)*
2 cloves garlic, finely chopped
1 loaf French bread, trimmed of crust and crumbled (about
    4 cups)
4 cups cold water
¼ cup red wine vinegar
Salt to taste
A few drops of Tabasco *(optional)*
¼ cup olive oil
1 tablespoon tomato paste

Put the cucumbers, tomatoes, onion, green pepper, garlic, and crumbled bread into a large bowl. Mix thoroughly. Stir in the water, vinegar, salt to taste, and Tabasco, if using. Blend the ingredients together in a blender or food processor, being careful to leave a little texture and not blending the soup until completely smooth. Stir in the olive oil and tomato paste, and whisk until completely mixed. Cover and refrigerate for at least 2 hours before serving.

NOTE: To prepare cucumbers, cut them in half lengthwise. Using a teaspoon, scrape out the seeds and discard them. Cut the cucumber flesh into pieces.
    To prepare the bell pepper, cut it in half from stem-top down and scoop out the seeds and discard. Cut the white ribs out and cut the halves into small pieces. ↷—.

VICHYSSOISE

⌐੭ This soup from Vichy, France, is usually served cold, but it also makes a hearty meal served hot with toasted buttered rye bread and sliced chilled tomatoes on the side. To make the best chilled Vichyssoise, you should plan ahead and refrigerate the soup, soup bowls, and spoons overnight.

4 tablespoons (½ stick) unsalted butter
4 leeks (white part only), cleaned and thinly sliced
    (about 3½ cups) *(see Note)*
1 medium onion, thinly sliced (about ⅔ cup)
2 teaspoons salt
1½ pounds russet potatoes, peeled and thinly sliced
    (about 4 cups)
4 cups chicken broth
4 cups milk
White pepper
Minced fresh chives for garnish

Melt the butter in a heavy-bottomed pan or a Dutch oven. Add the leeks and onion, and cook for 5 minutes, stirring occasionally to prevent scorching. Sprinkle with 1 teaspoon of the salt. Stir in the potatoes and cook for 1 minute. Add the chicken broth and the remaining 1 teaspoon salt. Cover and simmer for 30 minutes. Now scoop up the soup, one ladle at a time, and puree it in a blender or food processor. Return the soup to the pan, add the milk and a little white pepper, and bring to a boil. Boil for about 1 minute. Cool and refrigerate.

When ready to serve, taste the soup and correct the seasoning if necessary. Garnish with the minced chives.

NOTE: To clean a leek, cut off the stringy root end, and then cut the leek in half lengthwise. Hold it upside down with the root end closest to you, and run under cold water to wash away the sand and dirt. ᐁ

COLD CUCUMBER SOUP
WITH MINT

....

MAKES 4 CUPS

—◌ Think of this soup as "the colder, the better," especially on a warm summer evening. I like it best not overblended, when there are still some rough pieces of cucumber for texture.

2 cucumbers, peeled, seeded, and coarsely chopped
1 cup chicken broth
1/2 cup milk
1/2 cup cream
2 tablespoons lemon juice
Salt to taste
1 tablespoon finely chopped fresh mint
Sour cream, thinned with a little milk, for garnish

Put the cucumbers, chicken broth, milk, cream, and lemon juice into a blender or food processor. Pulse the ingredients together just until roughly blended; you will want to leave some pieces of cucumber unless you opt for a smoother consistency. Add salt to taste and the chopped mint, stirring with a spoon to mix.

Refrigerate for at least 1 hour before serving. Pour into chilled bowls or mugs, and garnish with a swirl of thinned sour cream. ◌—

CORN CHOWDER

....

—⁓ This is a supper soup that will make you smile—especially if you serve it with a sliced-heirloom-tomato salad.

3 slices bacon, chopped
2 onions, sliced
2 tablespoons butter
4 cups diced peeled potatoes (almost 1 pound)
2 tablespoons all-purpose flour
4 cups milk
2 cups frozen corn (or fresh if in season)
1 1/2 teaspoons salt
1 teaspoon black pepper
Whole nutmeg

Cook the bacon in a large soup pot until crisp. Add the onions and butter, and cook, stirring often, until the onions are golden brown, about 5 minutes. Put the potatoes in a separate pot, cover with cold water, and bring to a boil. Cook until the potatoes are tender when pierced with a fork; drain and set aside. Stir the flour into the onion and bacon mixture. As soon as the flour is blended smoothly into the mixture, slowly add the milk and stir until well blended and slightly thickened and smooth. Add the corn, potatoes, and seasonings to the soup, and cook for another 5 minutes.

When serving, grate a little nutmeg over each individual portion.

⁓

CIOPPINO

⟿ This dish will make you happy if you live in the San Francisco area. It is also good no matter where you live. It is a native San Francisco recipe that is a real winner. Make it once and it will be in your "favorite recipe" file forever. Serve it with bread that has a coarse crust.

1/2 cup olive oil
2 large onions, chopped *(see Note)*
3 carrots, peeled and chopped *(see Note)*
3 cloves garlic, mashed
4 cups tomato sauce
2 cups water
1 cup chopped fresh parsley
1 tablespoon crumbled dried basil
1 1/2 teaspoons crumbled dried thyme
3 pounds clams in shell, scrubbed *(see Note)*
2 pounds white fish fillets
2 crabs, cooked, cracked, and crabmeat removed *(optional)*
    (see Note)
1/4 cup dry white wine
Pinch of cayenne
Salt to taste

Heat the olive oil in a large kettle, add the onions, carrots, and garlic, and sauté until the onions are soft. Add the tomato sauce, water, parsley, basil, and thyme. Partially cover and simmer for 45 minutes. If the soup gets too thick, add a little more water. Add the clams and simmer for 10 minutes. Add the fish and crabmeat, if using, and simmer for 5 minutes. Stir in the wine, the cayenne, and salt to taste, and simmer for 10 minutes more.

To serve, ladle some of each variety of seafood into each bowl with a generous helping of broth.

NOTE: To prepare the onions, cut them in half through the root ends and remove the papery outside skin. Cut the onions into 1/4-inch slices lengthwise and 1/4-inch slices crosswise.

To prepare the carrots, trim off the tops and peel off the skin. Cut the carrots in half lengthwise and then cut crosswise into 1/4-inch pieces.

For the seafood, look for clams that are tightly closed. Once home, if a clam will not close when it's tapped lightly on a counter, discard it. If you are purchasing cooked crabs for the Cioppino, ask to smell them to ensure their freshness. They should not smell too fishy. In addition, most stores will crack them for you, making it much easier to remove the crab-meat.

SEAFOOD STEW

—◌ Seafood Stew was one of the all-time favorite recipes in many of the cooking classes that were given across the country in the late 1970s and early 1980s. The key to its success is brief cooking and making sure you buy fresh seafood. When I buy fish or seafood at the supermarket, I open the package as soon as I get into my car and smell the fish. If it doesn't have a pleasing aroma, I take it back into the store and return it. The seafood should smell "briny," not "fishy." The principle of this preparation is to use some of the seafood to make a full-flavored base and then add the rest of it to give the stew a lively fresh flavor.

1/2 cup olive oil
3 cloves garlic, minced
1 pound prawns or shrimp, shelled and deveined *(see Note)*
1 pound scallops
2 cups canned Italian tomatoes, with liquid (one 16-ounce can)
1 cup dry white wine
1 teaspoon crumbled dried oregano
1 teaspoon sugar
2 bay leaves, broken into several pieces
Salt and black pepper to taste
1 cup chopped fresh parsley

Pour the olive oil into a large sauté pan over medium heat. Add the garlic and cook for only 1 minute, stirring constantly so the garlic loses its rawness; if the garlic is browned, the taste will become acrid. Stir in 1/2 cup of the prawns and scallops combined. Chop the tomatoes roughly and add them and their liquid along with the wine, oregano, sugar, bay leaves, and salt and pepper to taste. Bring to a simmer, allowing the mixture to bubble gently. Cover and cook for 5 minutes. Add the remaining prawns and scallops, and cook for 2 minutes more. Remove from the heat and sprinkle in the parsley.

NOTE: To devein the prawns or shrimp, use the tip of a sharp knife to make a small cut down the back of each prawn from one end to the other and then remove the gray-black vein. Rinse the prawn with cold water. The intestinal vein contains grit and should always be removed. ⌒

THE IMPORTANCE OF FAMILY MEALS

Family meals should be more Norman Rockwell than Jerry Springer. If a family is too busy to have a family dinner . . . the result is a loss of family cohesion, solidarity, or people thinking of the family as a unit, "not a bunch of individuals doing their own thing." Families are where children learn "Who I am" and "Where I belong."

—Lisa M. Sodders, *Topeka Capital Journal*

CREAM OF TOMATO SOUP

....

MAKES 7 CUPS

—๑ Who doesn't remember this soup from childhood? There is nothing better than a warm bowl of Cream of Tomato Soup along with a few crackers to cure whatever is ailing you.

3 cups chopped peeled tomatoes (fresh, if in season,
    or canned) *(see Note)*
1/2 teaspoon baking soda
4 tablespoons (1/2 stick) butter
1/2 cup chopped onions
1/4 cup all-purpose flour
4 cups milk
1 tablespoon honey
11/2 teaspoons salt
1/2 teaspoon dried basil

Puree the tomatoes in a blender or food processor until smooth. Stir the baking soda into the tomatoes and set aside.

Melt the butter in a large soup pot. Add the onions and cook, stirring, over medium heat until the onions are softened but not browned. Sprinkle the flour over the onions and continue to cook and stir for 1 to 2 minutes. Slowly add the milk, honey, salt, and basil, and continue to cook and stir until slightly thickened. Stir in the pureed tomatoes and bring just to a simmer. Remove from the heat and push through a strainer using the back of a large spoon. Taste and correct the seasoning. Reheat before serving.

NOTE: The flavor of the tomatoes is critical to this soup. If garden-fresh tomatoes are not available or in season, canned tomatoes will give this soup more flavor. ๑—

THE PRIMAL RITE OF SOCIALIZATION

We may be witnessing the first generation in history that has not been required to participate in that primal rite of socialization, the family meal. The family meal is not only the core curriculum in the school of civilized discourse; it is also a set of protocols that curb our natural savagery and our animal greed, and cultivate a capacity for sharing and thoughtfulness.

Dinner rituals have nothing to do with class, or working women's busy lives, or any particular family structure. I've had dinners of boiled potatoes with families in Siberia, suppers of deli cold cuts with single welfare mothers in Chicago, bowls of watery gruel in the Sahara—all made memorable by the grace with which they were offered and by the sight of youngsters learning through experience the art of human companionship. However, all rituals involve, to some degree, a sacrifice, and the home meal requires genuine sacrifices of time and energy, large expenditures of those very traits it nurtures—patience, compassion, self-discipline.

—Francine du Plessix Gray, from an essay titled
"Starving Children" in *The New Yorker*

MULLIGATAWNY SOUP

⌒ This soup from India found its way into American cookery long before the Civil War. A recipe for it appeared in the original *Fannie Farmer Cookbook* of 1896. It is a soup that sparkles with flavor and will make a whole supper on a cold winter night.

4 tablespoons (¹/₂ stick) butter
1 onion, diced
1 carrot, peeled and diced
2 ribs celery with leaves, diced
1 green bell pepper, seeded, ribs removed, and diced
1 apple, peeled and grated
¹/₃ cup all-purpose flour
1 tablespoon curry powder
¹/₂ teaspoon ground nutmeg
6 cups chicken broth
1 cup chopped peeled tomatoes (fresh, if in season, or canned)
4 whole cloves, crushed
Salt and black pepper to taste
3 to 4 cups hot cooked white rice *(see page 117)*

Melt 2 tablespoons of the butter in a large soup pot. Add the onion, carrot, celery, green pepper, and grated apple, and simmer, stirring frequently, for about 15 minutes. Add the remaining 2 tablespoons butter to the pot. Mix the flour with the curry and nutmeg, add to the pot, and cook, stirring occasionally, over low heat for about 5 minutes. Stir in the broth, tomatoes, cloves, and salt and pepper to taste. Partially cover and simmer for 30 to 40 minutes. Taste and correct the seasoning.

To serve, place a mound of rice in each warmed soup bowl and ladle the soup into the bowl. Serve with a good crusty French bread.

VARIATION: You may add cooked chicken or fresh crab when in season for a more substantial soup. ᦂ

CHICKEN AND DUMPLING SOUP

—☙ Most Americans have memories of some relative preparing chicken and dumplings for them, either for a family gathering or for when they were under the weather. However, many people today have forgotten this timeless recipe. This version is full of flavor and very easy to prepare, so put it back in your recipe box and it will quickly become a family favorite again!

SOUP

One 3- to 4-pound chicken, in 8 pieces *(see page 121)*
2 carrots, peeled and sliced thin
2 ribs celery with leaves, sliced thin
1 large onion, chopped
2 teaspoons salt
1 1/2 teaspoons crumbled dried thyme
1/2 teaspoon crumbled dried rosemary
1/2 teaspoon black pepper

FEATHER DUMPLINGS

1 cup all-purpose flour
1/2 cup fresh bread crumbs
2 teaspoons baking powder
3/4 teaspoon salt
1/3 cup milk
1/4 cup finely chopped onion
1 egg, well beaten
2 tablespoons butter, melted
1 tablespoon finely minced fresh parsley
Black pepper to taste

To make the soup, rinse the chicken pieces, put them in a large pot, and add enough water to cover the chicken. Add the carrots, celery, onion, salt, thyme, rosemary, and pepper. Bring to a boil and reduce the heat to a simmer.

To make the feather dumplings, stir the flour, bread crumbs, baking powder, and salt in a mixing bowl. In another bowl, lightly beat the milk, onion, egg, and melted butter together, then stir into the dry ingredients to make a stiff batter. Add the parsley and pepper to taste and mix well.

When the chicken has simmered for 20 minutes, drop spoonfuls of the dough on top of the bubbling broth. Cover and steam for 20 minutes without lifting the lid. Taste the soup and add more salt and pepper if necessary. To serve, place a piece of chicken and a few dumplings in each soup bowl, then add enough broth to cover. ༄

HAM AND BEAN SOUP

⤙ Ham and Bean Soup holds a special place in my heart because it was one of my first and best lessons in cooking: Making it fancy won't make it better. Unfortunately, ham isn't what it used to be. It has lost some of its lively flavor. The addition of the Dijon mustard will help. You might want to add a little more, especially when reheating and serving for the second time.

1 pound (about 2 cups) Great Northern beans, soaked overnight
    and drained (yields 6 cups)
2 to 3 onions, chopped (about 2½ cups)
2 cups cut-up ham or smoked pork butt
¼ cup Dijon mustard (or to taste)
Salt and black pepper to taste

Put the beans, onions, and ham pieces in a large soup pot. Pour in enough cold water to cover the beans by 1½ inches and bring to a boil over medium heat. Reduce the heat to a simmer, removing any scum that rises to the surface. Simmer for about 2 hours, or until the beans are tender. Add more water if needed.

Stir in the mustard, then season with salt and pepper to taste. Skim off any fat that rises to the top and serve. ⤚

ANYTIME SPLIT PEA SOUP

SERVES 6

—∿ You can make this soup anytime, as long as you have on hand a few ordinary vegetables, a few dried herbs, and some green split peas. This soup is so good, you won't miss the ham (which is usually called for), but you can add some scraps if you like. Serve hot in bowls, with rye bread and a green salad.

8 cups cold water
1 pound (about 2 cups) green split peas
2 ribs celery, chopped
2 carrots, peeled and chopped
1 large onion, chopped
1/4 teaspoon dried thyme
1/4 teaspoon dried marjoram
1 bay leaf, crumbled
Salt and black pepper to taste

Put the cold water in a large soup pot and add all of the vegetables and herbs. Cover and boil for 20 minutes. Reduce the heat and simmer for about 30 minutes more, or until the split peas are very soft. Puree the soup in batches in a blender or food processor until smooth. Correct the seasoning, adding salt and pepper to taste. ∿—

TOMATO BREAD SOUP

⟳ Fresh tomatoes star in this soup, although canned tomatoes can easily replace them if tomatoes are out of season. The addition of bread to the soup as a thickener gives it a wonderful texture—leave some bread pieces chunkier if you prefer.

5 tablespoons olive oil
1 onion, sliced thin
1 1/2 to 2 cups chopped peeled tomatoes (fresh, if in season,
    or canned, with liquid)
One 6-ounce can tomato paste
7 cups water
4 cups chicken broth
1 loaf Italian bread (not sourdough), torn into pieces
    (about 4 cups)
3 large cloves garlic, chopped fine
1/4 cup chopped fresh basil, or 2 tablespoons dried
2 teaspoons kosher or coarse salt
Salt and black pepper to taste
Olive oil, to drizzle over top of soup when serving
Grated Parmesan cheese, to sprinkle on top when serving

Put the olive oil in a skillet and add the onion. Cook, stirring often, over medium heat until the onion is soft. Add the tomatoes and tomato paste, and cook, stirring often, over low heat for about 15 minutes. Heat the water with the chicken broth in a large soup pot. Add the bits of bread, garlic, basil, and kosher salt to the pot, and stir. Bring to a simmer and cook for about 5 minutes. Add the tomato mixture and stir together to blend. Puree the soup in a blender or food processor. Season with salt and pepper to taste. Serve hot with olive oil and Parmesan. ⟳

CREAM OF CELERY SOUP

⤚ Don't use the dark green outer ribs of the celery; the tender inner ribs have a better consistency and flavor for this soup.

4 tablespoons (1/2 stick) butter
6 ribs celery, chopped
1/3 cup chopped onion
2 cups chicken broth
1 1/2 cups light cream
Salt to taste

Put the butter in a soup pot and melt over medium-low heat. Add the celery and onion, and cook, stirring often, only until the vegetables are slightly softened, not browned. Add the broth and simmer for 30 minutes. Puree the soup in a blender or food processor. Return the soup to the pot and add the cream. Season with salt to taste.

Reheat slowly until very hot. Serve. ⤚

SIMPLE SUMMER
VEGETABLE SOUP

—⌀ Take advantage of summer's wonderful vegetables with this straightforward soup.

2 tablespoons butter
1 onion, chopped
2 carrots, peeled, quartered, and sliced
2 ribs celery, sliced
8 cups chicken broth
2 tomatoes, peeled and chopped
2 zucchini, quartered and sliced
1/2 cup string beans cut into 3-inch pieces, or peas
1 cup firmly packed fresh spinach leaves, washed and
     cut into strips
Salt and black pepper to taste

Melt the butter in a large soup pot; add the onion, carrots, and celery. Cook, stirring often, over medium heat for 5 minutes. Add the broth and tomatoes, and simmer for another 10 minutes. Stir in the zucchini and beans, and cook for another 2 minutes. Add the spinach and cook for 1 minute more. Season with salt and pepper to taste. ⌀

SIMPLE WINTER
VEGETABLE SOUP

....

⟿ Many people neglect the great vegetables of winter. Left to their simplicity in this soup, root vegetables have never tasted better.

2 tablespoons butter
2 onions, chopped
2 carrots, peeled, quartered, and sliced
8 cups chicken broth
1 russet potato, peeled and diced
1 turnip or medium-size rutabaga, peeled and cut into
    bite-sized wedges
1 celery root, peeled and diced
1 bay leaf, crumbled
1 teaspoon celery seed
Juice from 1/2 lemon
Salt and black pepper to taste

Melt the butter in a large soup pot; add the onions and carrots. Cook, stirring often, over medium heat for 5 minutes. Add the broth, potato, turnip, celery root, bay leaf, celery seed, and lemon juice, and simmer for 20 to 30 minutes, until the vegetables are nice and tender. Season with salt and pepper to taste. ↶

TURKEY SOUP

MAKES 10 CUPS

⌐⌐ Turkey bones alone don't do the trick for this soup. It's the leftover stuffing that gives it the flavor and body it needs. After tasting this soup, you'll find it's a great way to use your holiday leftovers.

1 turkey carcass, broken into pieces *(optional)*
11½ cups cold water
2½ cups leftover turkey stuffing
2 cups turkey gravy
3 carrots, peeled and thickly sliced
3 ribs celery with leaves, sliced
1 onion, chopped
½ cup chopped fresh parsley
1 bay leaf
2 teaspoons dried thyme, crumbled
Salt to taste

Put all the ingredients with 10 cups of the water in a large soup pot over medium heat, bring to a boil, and then reduce the heat to a simmer. Stir to break up all the clumps of stuffing, and mix well. Let the soup simmer for about 1½ hours. Add the remaining 1½ cups of cold water and let simmer for 10 more minutes. Taste for salt and adjust the flavoring if necessary. Serve hot. ⌐⌐

MUSTARD GREEN SOUP

I wish people were braver about using mustard greens. They are in almost every supermarket now. I remember driving around with my Italian mother and grandmother when I was growing up, and stopping by yellow fields to gather wild mustard greens, which we cooked with garlic and dressed with olive oil and vinegar. Navy beans blend well with the bite of bitter greens and are nice in this soup.

2 pounds turnips, peeled and diced
1/4 cup olive oil
1 large leek, cleaned and chopped, or 1 large onion, chopped
3 cloves garlic, finely chopped
2 cups cooked navy beans (canned are fine)
1/2 pound mustard greens (or any bitter greens), washed and
    coarsely chopped
6 cups chicken broth
Salt and black pepper to taste

Cook the turnips in a pot of boiling water for about 5 minutes to soften them. Drain and set aside. Heat the olive oil in a soup pot. Add the leek (or onion) and garlic, and cook, stirring often, over medium-low heat until the garlic and leek are softened but not browned. Stir in the turnips, beans, greens, and broth. Add salt and pepper to taste, and simmer for about 15 minutes. Serve hot.

OATMEAL SOUP

⌐ You will be surprised at how good this soup is and at how many enthusiastic responses you will get. It's a good soup to make when you have some leftover oatmeal from breakfast.

3 tablespoons butter
1 onion, chopped fine (about 3/4 cup)
1/2 cup uncooked oatmeal (not instant)
6 cups chicken broth
1 cup cooked oatmeal (follow package instructions)
Salt and black pepper to taste
3 tablespoons finely chopped fresh parsley

Melt the butter in a large saucepan over medium-low heat. Stir in the onion and cook, stirring often, just until the onion is soft. Add the uncooked oatmeal and stir constantly over medium-high heat (add a little more butter if needed) until the oatmeal is slightly golden. Stir in the chicken broth and mix well. Bring the broth to a simmer and add the cooked oatmeal, stirring until it is well mixed. Season with salt and pepper to taste, and cook at a simmer for 5 minutes. Add the parsley and serve. ⌐

BREAKING
BREAD
TOGETHER

Spoon Bread

Boston Brown Bread

Custard-Filled Corn Bread

Cream Biscuits

Rescue Biscuits

Bridge Creek Ginger Muffins

Popovers

Ice-Water Crackers

Crumpets

Raised Waffles

Refrigerator Rolls

Sally Lunn

Dewy Buns

Monkey Bread (Golden Monkey Ring)

Sticky Buns

Salt-Rising Bread

There is nothing like homemade breads, buns, and biscuits to make a meal special. They're not hard to make, and as they are baking, they fill the whole house with tempting smells.

If you've never made bread, you may want to start with the breads and biscuits in the beginning of this chapter that use baking powder as the leavener. But I urge you to take the plunge some rainy Sunday afternoon and get your hands into a yeast dough. It's not hard to make yeast-leavened breads—they just take longer. But you can always go off to the supermarket or for a swim while the dough is rising; it does not have to be watched.

The last recipe in this chapter, Salt-Rising Bread, *is* a bit more of a challenge, because you have to ferment the cornmeal and potato in order to create your own leavener. It's not hard to do, but how high your loaf may rise is somewhat unpredictable. But then, that's part of the fun, and you really feel you have created a bread from scratch.

SPOON BREAD

—☽ Many of our dearly loved home-cooked dishes are fading from memory, and they are not being replaced by better renditions. A perfect example of this is Spoon Bread. Spoon Bread was a frequent part of family meals for over a hundred years. Sarah Rutledge, author of *The Carolina Housewife*, written in 1847, gives a Spoon Bread recipe in her book and states, "Spoon Bread was as popular as a southern belle everywhere in the South." The apotheosis of corn bread—the ultimate, glorified idea—Spoon Bread is a steaming-hot, feather-light dish of cornmeal mixed with butter, eggs, and milk, lifted by the heat of the oven to a soufflé of airiness.

2¹/₂ cups water
1 cup yellow cornmeal
1 teaspoon salt
1 cup milk or buttermilk
4 eggs, well beaten
2 tablespoons butter

Preheat the oven to 400 degrees. Butter a 1¹/₂-quart casserole.
Stir ¹/₂ cup of cold water into the cornmeal. (This prevents lumping when the cornmeal is added to boiling water.) Bring 2 cups of water to a boil. Add the salt, then the cornmeal slowly, stirring constantly, and cook for 1 minute. Beat in the milk, eggs, and butter until smooth. Pour into the casserole and bake for about 40 minutes, or until a straw inserted in the center comes out clean. ☽

BOSTON BROWN BREAD

....

⁓ Boston Brown Bread is an old American steamed bread, moist and flavored with rye, molasses, and raisins. This old favorite can only be found today in cans on the supermarket shelf, a sad example of its past glory.

1 cup all-purpose flour
1 cup whole wheat flour
1/2 cup rye flour
1/2 cup yellow cornmeal
1 teaspoon baking soda
1 teaspoon baking powder
1 teaspoon salt
2 cups buttermilk
1 cup dark molasses
1 cup golden raisins

Before you begin to mix the ingredients together to make the batter, get the pot you are going to steam the bread in ready and grease the sides and bottoms of two empty 1-pound coffee cans. (You may choose to use two pots instead of one in order to fit a coffee can in each space.) The cans should stand on a rack so the water can circulate freely around the bottom. I sometimes use mason jar lids to keep the containers off the bottom if I don't have an extra rack. The pot must have a lid on top so the steam doesn't escape. Fill the pot with enough water to come halfway up the sides of the coffee cans. Start heating the water to bring it to a boil while you prepare the bread batter.

Put the all-purpose, whole wheat, and rye flours and the cornmeal into a large mixing bowl. Stir with a large spoon to mix well. Add the baking soda, baking powder, and salt, and stir to blend into the flours. Add the buttermilk and molasses, and briskly stir to blend everything thoroughly. Stir in the raisins. Pour the batter into the two well-greased cans, dividing it evenly between them. Each can will be about half full. Use a double layer of aluminum foil to snugly cover the tops, and secure the foil with rubber bands. Put the cans into the pot when the water is boiling, and cover the pot with a lid. Check occasionally to make sure there is enough water and that the water is boiling. Steam the breads for 2 hours. Remove the cans and take off the foil, then shake them upside down so the breads will slide out of the cans onto a rack. Let cool slightly before serving. ᕫ

CUSTARD-FILLED CORN BREAD

SERVES 8

⟶ I introduced a number of dishes to the breakfast menu of Berkeley's Bridge Creek Restaurant, which flourished in the eighties. Everyone particularly loved this cornbread with its surprise filling of creamy, soft custard. I first came across a version of this recipe in Marjorie Kinnan Rawlings's beguiling *Cross Creek Cookery*, published in 1942.

2 eggs
3 tablespoons butter, melted
3 tablespoons sugar
3/4 teaspoon salt
2 cups milk
1 1/2 tablespoons white vinegar
1 cup all-purpose flour
3/4 cup yellow cornmeal
1 teaspoon baking powder
1/2 teaspoon baking soda
1 cup corn kernels (about 2 ears corn)
1 cup heavy cream

Preheat the oven to 350 degrees. Butter an 8-inch square baking dish or pan that is about 2 inches deep. Put the buttered dish in the oven and let it get hot while you mix the batter.

Put the eggs in a mixing bowl and add the melted butter. Beat until well blended. Add the sugar, salt, milk, and vinegar, and beat well. Sift into a bowl or stir together in a bowl the flour, cornmeal, baking powder, and baking soda, then add to the egg mixture. Mix just until the batter is smooth and there are no lumps left. Stir in the corn kernels.

Pour the batter into the heated dish, then pour the cream into the center of the batter; don't stir. Bake for 50 minutes, or until lightly browned. Serve warm. ⟶

CREAM BISCUITS

—᪥ These biscuits are superior, and no student ever failed to make good ones in James Beard's cooking classes. They are better than most baking powder biscuits, and they are so ridiculously simple, you could probably make them blindfolded. They should be in your permanent recipe file. Cream Biscuits are ideal for Strawberry (or Peach) Shortcake *(page 190)*.

2 cups all-purpose flour
1 tablespoon baking powder
2 teaspoons sugar
1 teaspoon salt
1 to 1¹/₂ cups heavy cream
¹/₃ cup (5 tablespoons) butter, melted

Preheat the oven to 425 degrees. Have ready an ungreased baking sheet.

Toss together the flour, baking powder, sugar, and salt in a mixing bowl, stirring with a fork to blend and lighten. Slowly add 1 cup cream, stirring constantly. Gather the dough together; when it holds together and feels tender, it is ready to knead. If the dough seems shaggy and pieces are dry and falling away, slowly add enough additional cream to make the dough hold together.

Place the dough on a lightly floured surface and knead for 1 minute. Pat the dough into a square that is about ¹/₂ inch thick. Cut into 12 squares and dip each into the melted butter so all sides are coated. Place the biscuits 2 inches apart on the baking sheet. Bake for about 15 minutes, or until the biscuits are lightly browned. Serve hot. ᪥

RESCUE BISCUITS

—᠅ I call these Rescue Biscuits because they can save the day when your dinner has the blahs. They are quick to make, too.

3 cups all-purpose flour
2 tablespoons sugar
1 1/2 tablespoons baking powder
3/4 teaspoon cream of tartar
3/4 teaspoon salt
3/4 cup vegetable shortening
1 egg, lightly beaten
1 cup milk

Preheat the oven to 425 degrees.

Mix the flour, sugar, baking powder, cream of tartar, and salt together in a bowl. Cut in the shortening with a pastry blender just until the mixture resembles coarse meal. Lightly beat the egg and milk together. Add to the flour mixture all at once, stirring just enough with a fork to make a soft dough that sticks together.

Turn the dough out onto a lightly floured surface and knead gently 15 times. Roll out to a large square 1 inch thick. Cut into approximately 2-inch squares, and place them on an ungreased baking sheet. Bake for about 12 minutes, or until lightly browned. ᠅

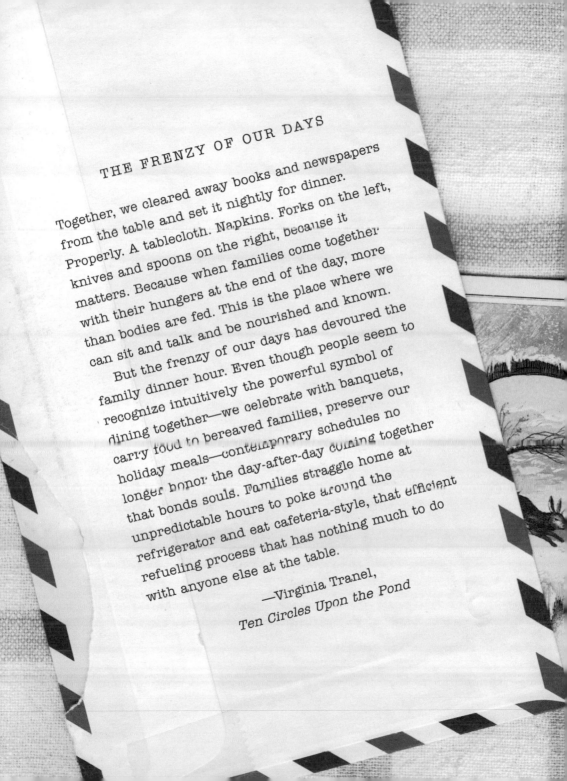

THE FRENZY OF OUR DAYS

Together, we cleared away books and newspapers from the table and set it nightly for dinner. Properly. A tablecloth. Napkins. Forks on the left, knives and spoons on the right, because it matters. Because when families come together with their hungers at the end of the day, more than bodies are fed. This is the place where we can sit and talk and be nourished and known.

But the frenzy of our days has devoured the family dinner hour. Even though people seem to recognize intuitively the powerful symbol of dining together—we celebrate with banquets, carry food to bereaved families, preserve our holiday meals—contemporary schedules no longer honor the day-after-day coming together that bonds souls. Families straggle home at unpredictable hours to poke around the refrigerator and eat cafeteria-style, that efficient refueling process that has nothing much to do with anyone else at the table.

—Virginia Tranel,
Ten Circles Upon the Pond

BRIDGE CREEK
GINGER MUFFINS

....

MAKES 16 MUFFINS

—◌ Don't overlook these muffins. Since fresh ginger is so readily available today, I took this old recipe and transformed it by using the fresh root, which gives the muffins a very lively, pleasing taste.

2 ounces unpeeled fresh ginger
3/4 cup plus 3 tablespoons sugar
2 tablespoons lemon peel, including some white pith
    (from 2 lemons)
8 tablespoons (1 stick) butter, softened
2 eggs
1 cup buttermilk
2 cups all-purpose flour
1/2 teaspoon salt
3/4 teaspoon baking soda

Preheat the oven to 375 degrees. Grease 16 muffin cups.

Cut the unpeeled ginger into large chunks. If you have a food processor, process the ginger until it is in tiny pieces; or hand chop the ginger into fine pieces. You should have 1/4 cup. It is better to have too much ginger than too little. Put the ginger and 1/4 cup of the sugar in a small skillet or saucepan and cook over medium heat until the sugar has melted and the mixture is hot. Don't walk away from the pan—this cooking takes only a couple of minutes. Remove from the stove and let the ginger mixture cool.

Put the lemon peel and the 3 tablespoons sugar in the food processor and process until the lemon peel is in small bits; or chop the lemon peel by hand and then add the sugar. Add the ginger mixture and stir to combine.

Put the butter in a mixing bowl and beat a second or two; add the remaining 1/2 cup sugar and beat until smooth. Add the eggs and beat well. Add the buttermilk and mix until blended. Add the flour, salt, and baking soda, and mix until smooth. Add the ginger-lemon mixture and mix well.

Spoon the batter into the muffin tins so that each cup is three-quarters full. Bake for 15 to 20 minutes. Serve warm. ✑

POPOVERS

⎯ ⌒ The glory of popovers is their incredible size, crusty out-sides, and tender, creamy, almost hollow insides just waiting for butter and a spoonful of strawberry jam. But I had about given up on making them over the last few years because they kept turning out to be sullen little muffins—pop*unders*. I had forgot-ten that popovers rise highest when they get a forceful amount of heat quickly, and I had been using muffin tins instead of separate containers like ovenproof Pyrex glass baking cups, which work perfectly. I had a thrill when I opened the oven door and my popovers were once again giant golden balloons. Popovers are meant to go with chicken, roasts, salads, and soups; they don't belong with spaghetti, curries, or chili.

$1^{1}/_{2}$ cups all-purpose flour
$1^{1}/_{2}$ cups milk
3 eggs
3 tablespoons butter, melted
1 teaspoon salt

Preheat the oven to 425 degrees. Grease seven $^{3}/_{4}$-cup-sized Pyrex glass cups, or 7 small ramekins.

Beat the flour, milk, eggs, melted butter, and salt together until smooth. I use a blender, but a rotary beater works fine, too. Fill the cups almost to the top. Place the cups on a baking sheet so they are not touch-ing, and put them in the oven. Bake for about 30 minutes, or until the popovers are golden and light. Lift one out of its cup, and if it feels light, it is done. Serve immediately. I rather like these popovers when they have fallen and been rewarmed. Reheated, they get some of their puffi-ness back. ⌒

LOST RECIPES / 42

ICE-WATER CRACKERS

—෩ While it is hard to beat a store-bought saltine for crispness and pleasant good taste, it is possible to give that same saltine a different and delicious personality by dipping it in ice water, spreading it with melted butter, and baking it again. Puffy, buttery, and done to a deep golden brown, this reinvented cracker is especially good with soups and chowders.

Lillian Marshall, an outstanding Kentucky cook and author, does imaginative things with food, and this is one of them.

24 saltine crackers
8 cups ice water
8 tablespoons (1 stick) unsalted butter, melted

Preheat the oven to 400 degrees. (If using a convection oven, reduce the heat by 50 degrees.)

Place the saltines in a shallow baking pan in a single layer and pour the ice water over them. Let stand for about 3 minutes. Carefully remove the crackers with a slotted spoon or spatula and place on a double layer of paper towels (laid over a kitchen towel) to drain for 5 to 8 minutes. Dry the pan and pour half of the melted butter over the bottom; spread the butter out with your fingers. Arrange the crackers on the buttered pan and drizzle the remaining butter over them.

Place in the hot oven and bake for 15 to 20 minutes. Check frequently; don't let the crackers burn. Serve hot. ෩

CRUMPETS

—෴ An old English teatime treat, crumpets are just as good for breakfast, served with lots of butter and honey or jam. It's nice to see them making a comeback today.

1 package active dry yeast
¹/4 cup warm water
1 teaspoon sugar
1¹/2 cups milk, warmed
2 cups all-purpose flour
1 teaspoon salt
1 teaspoon baking soda
¹/4 cup warm water

Sprinkle the yeast over the warm water in a large mixing bowl. Add the sugar, stir, and let the yeast dissolve for about 5 minutes. Add the milk, flour, and salt, and beat until smooth. Cover the bowl with plastic wrap and let stand for 1 hour (if you want to make the batter the night before, cover and refrigerate overnight). Stir down. Dissolve the baking soda in the warm water and stir into the batter. Cover and let rest for 30 minutes.

Heat a griddle or a heavy frying pan and grease some 3-inch rings (you can use 6¹/2-ounce tuna-type cans with tops and bottoms cut out). When the griddle is medium-hot, grease it and place the rings on it. Spoon about 3 tablespoons of batter into each ring, just enough to cover the bottom. Lower the heat and cook slowly on the griddle for about 8 minutes, or until the tops of the crumpets have lost their shine and are dull and holey. Remove the rings and set aside the crumpets. When you've finished the batch, toast the crumpets, butter them generously, and serve. ෴

RAISED WAFFLES

—❧ This recipe comes from the 1896 *Fannie Farmer Cookbook*. The Raised Waffle recipe alone could have sold a million copies. Don't make the mistake of thinking this is just another waffle; it isn't. It has won more accolades than any recipe I know, and it deserves them all. This is a recipe that uses yeast, but you don't have to knead the dough; you simply leave it in a warm place overnight, and it's just about ready to be baked the next morning.

Waffles aren't just for breakfast. In the past they were often eaten for lunch or supper, with creamed chicken, turkey, or ham.

1/2 cup warm water
1 package active dry yeast
2 cups milk, warmed
8 tablespoons (1 stick) butter, melted
1 teaspoon salt
1 teaspoon sugar
2 cups all-purpose flour
2 eggs
1/4 teaspoon baking soda

Use a rather large mixing bowl—the batter will rise to double its original volume. Put the water in the mixing bowl and sprinkle in the yeast. Let stand for 5 minutes to dissolve. Add the milk, melted butter, salt, sugar, and flour to the yeast mixture and beat until smooth and well blended (I often use a hand rotary beater to get rid of the lumps). Cover the bowl with plastic wrap and let stand overnight at room temperature.

Just before cooking the waffles, beat in the eggs, add the baking soda, and stir until well mixed. The batter will be very thin. Pour about 1/2 to 3/4 cup batter into a very hot waffle iron. Bake the waffles until they are golden and crisp. This batter will keep well for several days in the refrigerator. ❧

REFRIGERATOR ROLLS

MAKES 16 ROLLS

—↶ These are known as Refrigerator (or Icebox) Rolls because once the dough is made, you can store it in the refrigerator for about a week, ready to use whenever you need it. If you are like most people and are making the rolls for company, follow the directions below for shaping and baking them. You could also make a nice White Loaf—see Note at the end of this recipe.

1 cup milk, warmed
2 packages active dry yeast
3 tablespoons sugar
2 teaspoons salt
2 tablespoons melted butter
1 egg, lightly beaten
2½ or more cups all-purpose flour

Stir the warm milk and yeast together in a large mixing bowl and let stand for a couple of minutes to dissolve the yeast. Add the sugar, salt, melted butter, egg, and 2 cups of the flour. Beat to mix well, and then add enough additional flour to make a manageable dough. Turn the dough out onto a lightly floured surface, knead for about 2 minutes, then let rest for 10 minutes. Resume kneading until the dough is smooth and elastic, about 8 minutes, sprinkling on just enough additional flour to keep the dough from being too sticky. Place in a large greased bowl, cover, and let rise until doubled in bulk. You may also refrigerate it overnight.

If you have refrigerated the dough overnight, let it come to room temperature. Remove from the bowl, and on a lightly floured work surface, punch the dough down and cut it into 4 even-sized pieces using a knife or metal scraper. Cut each of the 4 dough pieces into 4 even-sized pieces. Shape each piece by flattening it and folding each corner into the center. Turn the piece of dough over and shape it into a round ball. With your palm, roll each ball in a circular motion. Place the rolls evenly apart on a greased baking sheet and loosely cover with plastic wrap. Let rise for about 20 minutes while the oven preheats to 400 degrees. Bake for about 15 minutes, or until lightly browned. Remove from the pan and let cool on a rack.

NOTE: To make a White Loaf, pat and shape the dough into a ball after its first rising, then plop it into a greased 8½ by 4½-inch loaf pan, patting it to spread it out to fill the pan. Bake in a preheated 350-degree oven for 40 minutes.

SALLY LUNN

....

⎯◌ A lovely, butter-rich cake or bun. The story goes that Sally Lunn, a resident of eighteenth-century Bath, England, peddled these small cakes on the streets, and a local baker was so impressed that he not only bought her business but composed a song about her. Leftovers are good toasted for breakfast and served with your favorite preserves.

1 cup milk, cream, or evaporated milk
8 tablespoons (1 stick) butter
1 package active dry yeast
1/3 cup sugar
1 1/2 teaspoons salt
4 eggs
3 3/4 cups all-purpose flour

Pour the milk into a small saucepan, and then add the butter, cut into tablespoon bits. Place over low heat until the butter is melted, then pour into a large mixing bowl and let cool to lukewarm. Sprinkle on the yeast, sugar, and salt; stir, and let stand for 5 minutes, until the yeast dissolves. Add the eggs one by one and beat until completely blended. Add the flour, about 1 cup at a time, beating after each addition until the batter is perfectly smooth. Cover the bowl and let the batter rise until doubled in bulk—about 3 hours or more.

Butter a 10-inch tube pan or 24 muffin cups. Beat the risen batter well to deflate it, then pour it into the tube pan or spoon it into the muffin cups, filling each cup about half full. Use your buttered fingers to spread the batter evenly and smooth the top. Cover loosely with a towel and let rise again until doubled in bulk.

Bake in a preheated 375-degree oven, allowing about 50 minutes for the tube bread or about 20 minutes for the small buns, until well browned on top. Remove from the pan and turn out onto a rack to cool.

Notes from a Scandinavian Kitchen

We want to do more with less. World hunger is appalling. Plastic throwaways glut our valleys. Convenience foods give off no warming kitchen aromas. We don't long for the past, but we ache for that part of it that can enrich our living today. A heritage is preserved, it's nourished. It grows from bits and pieces told and written. But it lives through use.

—Morry and Florence Ekstrand,
Notes from a
Scandinavian Kitchen

DEWY BUNS

MAKES 20 BUNS

—ᗌ You may agree with the saying "Man cannot live by bread alone," unless you happen to be eating a Dewy Bun. I ate my first Dewy Bun in Pennsylvania Dutch Country at the Lancaster Market, and if you are thinking of changing careers, a Dewy Bun business could make you rich. These light plump buns filled with vanilla custard are so good, I bet you can't eat just one.

2 packages active dry yeast
1/3 cup warm water
1 1/2 cups milk
1/3 cup vegetable shortening
1/4 cup sugar
2 teaspoons salt
2 eggs, lightly beaten
4 1/2 cups all-purpose flour
Custard Filling (recipe follows)

Sprinkle the yeast over the warm water in a large mixing bowl and let it dissolve for 5 minutes. Put the milk and shortening in a saucepan and heat until the shortening is melted. Let cool to lukewarm.

Pour the cooled milk mixture over the yeast, then stir in the sugar, salt, eggs, and 2 cups of the flour. Beat briskly until well blended. Add the remaining 2 1/2 cups flour and beat until smooth. Cover the bowl and let the dough double in bulk. At this point, if you want to leave the dough overnight, cover the bowl with plastic wrap and put it in the refrigerator.

If you are proceeding immediately, when the dough has doubled in bulk, dust a work surface generously with flour and turn the dough onto it. This is a soft dough and needs enough flour on the work surface to prevent sticking. Pat the dough out into a circle if you are making round

LOST RECIPES / 50

buns, or into a square about ¹/₂ inch thick if you want square buns. Use a biscuit cutter for round buns, and cut the dough into 2¹/₂-inch squares for square buns. (If you have left the dough in the refrigerator overnight, it will take time to double in bulk, often a couple of hours at room temperature to warm up and begin to rise. When it has doubled, proceed as directed above.)

Preheat the oven to 425 degrees. Grease a baking sheet.

Cut out the buns and place them on the baking sheet, 1 inch apart. They don't spread much, they rise. Let the buns rest and rise on the baking sheet for 20 minutes, uncovered. Bake for about 10 minutes; watch carefully so they don't get too brown. They should be just golden. Remove and let cool a little. Split only as many buns as you are going to serve and spread each with about 2 tablespoons custard. (If the custard has been in the refrigerator, bring it to room temperature before using.)

Freeze the buns you have left to be used later. Ideally, the buns should be warm when served. They are perfect this way. ↭

CUSTARD FILLING
MAKES 1 ¹/₄ CUPS

1 cup milk
¹/₃ cup sugar
3 tablespoons cornstarch
¹/₈ teaspoon salt
2 eggs, lightly beaten
1¹/₂ tablespoons butter
1 teaspoon vanilla

Heat the milk in a heavy saucepan over medium-high heat until bubbles form a ring around the edge of the pan. Meanwhile, mix the sugar, cornstarch, and salt together in a bowl. When the milk has formed bubbles (or is scalded, as it is described in old cookbooks), slowly pour it over the sugar mixture. Stir briskly until smooth. Pour the mixture back into the saucepan and cook over medium heat, stirring until thickened. This should take 3 to 5 minutes. Taste the custard and if it is smooth, take it off the heat. Add ½ cup of the custard to the eggs, stirring rapidly so the hot custard doesn't cook the eggs. Stir the egg mixture into the custard in the pan and put it back on the heat. Cook, stirring constantly, for another 2 to 3 minutes. When the custard is smooth, remove from the heat and add the butter and vanilla; stir to blend. Let cool a little, cover, and refrigerate until needed. ℘

A New Definition of the Human Being

If you take away from food the wholeness of growing it or take away the joy and conviviality of preparing it in your own home, then I believe you are talking about a whole new definition of the human being.

Wendell Berry, The Unsettling of America

MONKEY BREAD (GOLDEN MONKEY RING)

MAKES ONE 10-INCH TUBE LOAF

—◠ A spectacular-looking breakfast bread, made by piling up small rounds of dough, all held together with a goocy sugar-and-butter mixture. The finished loaf, when turned out of the pan, is easily pulled apart into separate rolls.

Sweet-Roll Dough (recipe follows)
1 cup granulated sugar
3/4 cup packed dark brown sugar
8 tablespoons (1 stick) butter, melted

Prepare the dough. After it has had its first rising, punch it down and let rest for about 10 minutes.

Mix the granulated sugar and brown sugar together, and spread out on a large plate or piece of waxed paper. Grease a 10-inch tube pan quite generously.

Have the melted butter slightly warm. Tear off golf-ball-sized pieces of dough (you should have about 30), and with your lightly floured hands, roll them into round balls. Dip about 6 of the balls into the melted butter, then roll them in the sugar mixture, turning them until they are completely coated. Place the balls in the prepared pan, leaving about 1/2 inch between them. Now you should stop and wash your hands—otherwise they get so sticky, it's difficult to work.

Dip about 6 more balls into the butter and roll them in the sugar mixture, then place them in the pan. Continue filling the pan by layering the buttered and sugared balls of dough (and stopping to wash your hands, too). When all the dough is used up, sprinkle any remaining sugar mixture over the top, cover *loosely* with aluminum foil, and let the dough rise to the top of the pan.

Bake in a preheated 350-degree oven for about 1 hour. If the top begins to brown too much, cover loosely with a piece of foil and continue baking. Remove from the oven and let cool in the pan for 10 minutes. Unmold onto a large platter if you are serving warm, or onto a rack if you want the bread to cool completely. ༳

SWEET-ROLL DOUGH

—༳ This is a first-rate basic sweet dough. It has a fine, slightly dense texture, and it's richer than other dough recipes.

2 packages active dry yeast
1/4 cup warm water
1 cup milk, warmed
8 tablespoons (1 stick) butter, softened
3 eggs *(see Note)*
1/2 cup sugar
2 teaspoons salt
51/4 to 53/4 cups all-purpose flour

Sprinkle the yeast over the warm water in a small cup or bowl, stir, and let stand for 5 minutes, until the yeast dissolves. Put the milk, butter, eggs, sugar, and salt in a large mixing bowl and beat well. Stir in the dissolved yeast. Add 21/2 cups of the flour, and beat until smooth and well blended. Add 21/2 cups more flour and beat until the dough holds together in a rough, shaggy mass. Turn out onto a lightly floured surface and knead for a minute or two. Let rest for 10 minutes.

Resume kneading for 8 to 10 minutes more, gradually sprinkling on a little more flour if the dough sticks to your hands, until smooth and elastic. Place in a greased bowl, cover with plastic wrap, and let rise in a warm place until doubled in bulk.

Punch the risen dough down. It is now ready to be formed and baked for the Monkey Bread or Sticky Buns *(page 56)*. You can also freeze the dough at this point, or store in the refrigerator for a few days in a tightly covered container.

NOTE: If the eggs are refrigerator cold, pour hot water over them and let stand for several minutes to warm before cracking. ∽

STICKY BUNS

∙∙

MAKES 24 BUNS

DOUGH

Sweet-Roll Dough *(page 54)*

CARAMEL GLAZE

12 tablespoons (1½ sticks) butter, softened
1½ cups packed brown sugar
3 tablespoons dark corn syrup

FILLING

6 tablespoons (¾ stick) butter, melted
1 cup packed light brown sugar
½ cup chopped nuts
½ cup raisins

Prepare the dough and set aside to rise.

To make the caramel glaze, beat the softened butter, brown sugar, and corn syrup together until thoroughly mixed. Spread evenly over the buttered bottoms of three 8-inch round cake or pie pans (or a combination of pie and cake pans).

After the dough has had its first rising, roll it on a floured surface to a rectangle about 32 by 12 inches and ⅓ inch thick. Brush the surface with the melted butter. Mix together thoroughly the brown sugar, nuts, and raisins. Sprinkle evenly over the buttered dough and press in gently with your fingers. Beginning with a long side, roll the dough up like a jelly roll, then cut it into pieces about 1¼ inches wide—you should have 24 slices. Place 8 pieces, cut side down, in each of the prepared pans, putting 7 around the edge and 1 in the middle. Press the pieces down gently so they just touch. Cover and let rise until puffy, swollen, and doubled in bulk.

Bake in a preheated 375-degree oven for about 25 minutes, or until golden brown on top. Remove from the oven and let cool in the pans for 5 minutes so the glaze will set, then invert onto serving boards or platters; some of the glaze will dribble over the sides. Serve warm.

HUMANS HAVE ALWAYS COOKED

The preparing, cooking, and sociable eating of food are so central to the human experience that the culinary arts may well be what made us human in the first place.... There is no record anywhere of any people who have lived without cooking.

—Richard W. Wrangham,
Professor of Anthropology
at Harvard University

SALT-RISING BREAD

....

—⌒ Salt-Rising Bread is a great adventure to make—and worth it because you cannot find anything like it in supermarkets or even bakeries. It is rather dense and heavy, with a creamy texture and a wonderful "cheesy" taste and aroma. It will not rise quite as high as other yeast breads, but its rather compact, chewy texture makes it fabulous for toasting, and it makes the best grilled-cheese sandwiches you've ever had.

The name "Salt-Rising Bread" stems from the original method of keeping the dough warm: The bowl of dough was set in a large container of warmed rock salt, which held the heat for a long time. It's no longer necessary to keep the dough warm with salt, although it does need to be kept warmer than conventional yeast doughs—at about 100 degrees. In the recipe, I've given suggestions for convenient warm places found in almost every home. You must use a nondegerminated cornmeal—such as a true stone-ground cornmeal found in health-food stores—which keeps the germ in the milling process.

The finished loaves freeze well and are wonderful to have on hand.

STARTER

2 medium-size potatoes, peeled and thinly sliced
4 cups boiling water
1/4 cup nondegerminated cornmeal, such as stone-ground
 (see above)
2 tablespoons sugar
1 teaspoon salt

1¹/₂ cups milk
The above starter
¹/₄ teaspoon baking soda
4 cups all-purpose flour

BREAD DOUGH

5 to 6 cups all-purpose flour
2¹/₂ teaspoons salt
6 tablespoons vegetable shortening
The above sponge

To make the starter, put the potatoes in a large bowl, pour the boiling water over them, then stir in the cornmeal, sugar, and salt. Place the bowl in a larger bowl of hot water, and set in a warm place where the temperature remains fairly steady. (A gas oven with the interior light on or the top of the water heater are both good places.)

Replace the hot water in the larger bowl 2 or 3 times—or whenever you think of it and it's convenient—over the next 24 hours. Then remove the potato slices from the bowl, discard them, and continue on with the sponge.

To make the sponge, heat the milk until it is comfortably warm to your finger, then add it to the starter, along with the baking soda and the flour. Beat briskly until smooth—a hand rotary beater works particularly well to help smooth out the lumps. Cover with plastic wrap and again place in a larger bowl of hot water. Set in a warm place, and let the sponge double in bulk—this usually takes 2 to 3 hours, but check it after 1¹/₂ hours. When doubled, the dough will look creamy and light. Don't let it sit longer after it has become creamy and light, or it will lose its "cheesy" flavor and become sour.

To make the bread dough, put 4 cups of the flour in a large bowl. Add the salt and mix lightly with a fork. Drop in the shortening and blend it in with your fingers—as though you were making pie dough—until the mixture looks like fine meal. Add the flour mixture to the sponge and beat until well mixed. Add enough flour—1 to 2 more cups—to make a soft, manageable dough you can knead. Turn out onto a floured surface and knead for a minute or two. Let rest for 10 minutes.

Resume kneading and continue until the dough is smooth (this dough is heavy and rather puttylike)—about 10 minutes. Divide into thirds and shape each piece into a loaf. Place the loaves in three greased 8½ by 4½-inch loaf pans. Cover loosely with plastic wrap, set the pans in a larger pan of hot water, and again set in a warm place to rise. This final rise will take about 3 hours, and the loaves should increase in volume by about one-third (less than the usual doubling).

Bake in a preheated 350-degree oven for 45 to 55 minutes, until golden brown. If in doubt, it's better to bake the loaves a few minutes longer than to underbake. Turn out of the pans and let cool on a rack.

VEGETABLES WITH A FINISH

Cold Asparagus with Sesame Mayonnaise

Garlic-Crumb-Stuffed Artichokes

A Side Dish of Onions

Scalloped Spinach

Scalloped Potatoes

Southern Green Beans

Creamed Corn

Baked Squash with Butter and
Maple Syrup

Filled Green Peppers

Candied Carrots

Sugared Beets

Rainy Day Vegetable Cobbler

Succotash

Vegetable Barley

Broccoli in Cheese Custard

Colcannon

In the past, vegetables used to be dressed up a little more. Today we usually just blanch them briefly or sauté them quickly, and they are served crisp and under-cooked. But there are some lovely lost recipes that give vegetables a nice finish—bringing out the flavors of carrots, beets, onions, and winter squash, for instance, by glazing them with a little sugar or maple syrup; making a scalloped dish by baking vegetables in a custard or a cream sauce; and stuffing certain vegetables for a more substantial dish.

I remember how my grandmother used to stuff artichokes. My grandmother, who was Italian, spent most of her waking hours in the kitchen. When she wasn't cooking, she would sit at the kitchen table knitting or sewing. She never learned to speak English, but her cooking spoke for her and it was wonderful—particularly the artichokes she lovingly stuffed with bread crumbs.

So here are some of those old-fashioned vegetable dishes. They are particularly good for the home cook because they can be prepared ahead and reheated quickly, so there is no last-minute draining of steaming pots of water while everyone is at the table waiting.

COLD ASPARAGUS WITH SESAME MAYONNAISE

‌◦> Cold cooked asparagus served with mayonnaise for dipping seems to have fallen off menus and has been forgotten by home cooks. However, the combination of flavors is still divine. I've updated this classic by adding sesame oil to the mayonnaise.

2 pounds asparagus
1/2 to 1 teaspoon toasted sesame oil
1/3 cup mayonnaise

Wash the asparagus and cut off the tough, woody bottoms of each stalk and discard. Bring a large pot of salted water to a boil and drop in the asparagus. Depending on how thick the stalks are, cook for 2 to 5 minutes. To test for doneness, pick up a stalk with tongs: It should just droop slightly. Be careful not to overcook. With tongs, remove the asparagus from the water and let cool to room temperature. Cover and refrigerate until serving time.

To make the sesame mayonnaise, mix 1/2 teaspoon sesame oil into the mayonnaise and stir well to blend. Continue to add more oil until the flavor suits you. Serve each portion of asparagus with a scant tablespoon of mayonnaise on the side. ◦◦—

GARLIC-CRUMB-STUFFED ARTICHOKES

....

SERVES 4

—ᦞ Many people serve these warm, but I like them cold. I usually prepare the artichokes up to a day ahead, wrap them well, and refrigerate until serving. They make a good substitute for the usual salad. Note that each slice of bread makes approximately ¼ cup when crumbed. Each artichoke takes about ¼ cup of crumbs to stuff. And don't detach the stems from the artichokes until after cooking; they are very good.

4 artichokes
4 slices bread
2 large cloves garlic, finely chopped
¾ teaspoon salt
6 tablespoons olive oil

Bring a large pot of water to a boil. Peel the coarse fibers from the artichoke stems. Remove the tough bottom leaves, then slice 1 inch off the top of each artichoke. With scissors, snip off the prickly tops of the remaining side leaves. Drop the artichokes into the boiling water, and boil them gently until the bottoms of the chokes are tender when pierced with a fork, 15 to 20 minutes. Remove the artichokes from the water and turn them upside down on a large plate to drain.

While the artichokes are cooking, prepare the crumbs. Tear each slice of bread into 5 or 6 pieces and put them in a blender or food processor. Blend a few seconds until you have crumbs. Spread the crumbs on a baking sheet and dry them in a 250-degree oven until lightly golden, about 15 minutes.

Toss together the crumbs, garlic, salt, and olive oil in a bowl to mix well.

Using your fingers, separate the artichoke leaves so they open up a little. Spoon a small amount (about 1 teaspoon) of stuffing between the leaves until it is all used up. Serve warm or chilled. ∾

ROUSSEAU'S PARADOX

In every city dweller there is a displaced yearning for the rustic farm and land, the taste of the homegrown, all the natural foods. The paradox is that we do want authentic country flavors and integrity, but we do not seek the discomforts of the simple life, so we rediscover regionalism vicariously amid modern convenience and luxury.

—Jean-Jacques Rousseau

A SIDE DISH OF ONIONS

⟶ I can't think of a better side dish than these buttered sweet onions. The brown sugar will caramelize, bringing out the natural sweetness of the onions. Serve them with roasted chicken, pork tenderloin, or your favorite hamburgers.

2 pounds small white onions
4 tablespoons (1/2 stick) butter, melted
3 tablespoons light brown sugar
1 tablespoon Dijon mustard
1 1/2 teaspoons salt
1/4 teaspoon black pepper
1/3 cup chopped fresh parsley

Preheat the oven to 350 degrees.

Bring a large pot of water to a boil. Drop the onions into the boiling water and cook for 3 minutes; drain and remove the outer skins.

Place the onions in a buttered shallow 1-quart baking dish. Combine the butter, brown sugar, mustard, salt, and pepper, and pour over the onions.

Bake the onions until they are browned and well heated throughout, 20 to 40 minutes. After 20 minutes, taste an onion to see if it is done. Sprinkle with parsley before serving. ⟶

SCALLOPED SPINACH

‑‑ᴄᴏ Rich, creamy Scalloped Spinach is a natural accompaniment to red meat. Although some recipes omit the bacon, adding pieces of cooked bacon balances the flavor of this recipe.

4 slices bacon, chopped
1 onion, chopped
2 eggs
2 cups cooked chopped spinach (2 bunches fresh or
    two 10-ounce boxes frozen)
2 tablespoons all-purpose flour
1¹/₂ cups milk
³/₄ cup cracker crumbs, such as saltines
2 tablespoons butter

Preheat the oven to 350 degrees. Grease an 8 by 3-inch casserole.

Cook the chopped bacon in a skillet over medium-high heat until crisp. Add the onion and fry until tender but not browned, about 3 minutes.

Beat the eggs in a large bowl, then add the cooked spinach, flour, and milk; stir until well mixed. Add the cooked bacon and onion and mix together. Pour into the casserole and cover the top with the cracker crumbs. Dot with butter and bake for 15 to 20 minutes, until browned.

SCALLOPED POTATOES

⁓ Little rivers of buttery milk, lots of pepper, and creamy potatoes.

4 medium potatoes, peeled and sliced 1/4 inch thick
Salt and black pepper to taste
3 tablespoons all-purpose flour
4 tablespoons (1/2 stick) butter
About 1 1/2 cups milk

Preheat the oven to 350 degrees. Butter a 1 1/2-quart casserole.

Cover the bottom of the casserole with a single layer of potatoes. Sprinkle generously with salt and pepper, flour, and a few dots of the butter. Repeat until all the potato slices are used. Before dotting the final layer with butter, pour the milk over the potato slices until the top is almost covered. Dot with the remaining butter. Bake for 1 hour, or until the potatoes are soft.

SCALLOPED POTATOES WITH CELERY ROOT (CELERIAC): Use only 2 potatoes and alternate each layer of potatoes with a layer of peeled, thinly sliced celery root. ⁓

SOUTHERN GREEN BEANS

—◌ For the past few years, most of us have been following the recommended way of cooking green beans until just tender, because we've been told that long cooking destroys flavor and vitamins. But these green beans, with potatoes and a hint of bacon, have a fullness of flavor and depth of character that crunchy beans just don't have.

3 or 4 slices smoky-style bacon, diced
1 pound green beans, washed, ends trimmed, and cut into
     1-inch lengths
Salt and black pepper to taste
1 cup water
2 scallions, sliced
2 medium potatoes, peeled and diced

Heat a Dutch oven or heavy-bottomed pot with a lid. Add the bacon and cook over medium-low heat until lightly browned, about 5 minutes. Add the green beans, salt and pepper, and water. Cover and cook over medium low heat for about 10 minutes. Add the scallions and potatoes, stir to mix, cover, and cook for 30 minutes more. Check once or twice to make sure the liquid hasn't all evaporated. Serve hot. ◌

CREAMED CORN

—◌ Eating an ear of friendly corn always reminds me of how down-to-earth and pleasing this native American vegetable is.

5 ears sweet corn (about 2½ cups corn kernels), husks and
    silk removed
1 tablespoon butter
¼ cup thinly sliced scallions, or diced shallots
½ cup half-and-half, heavy cream, or crème fraîche
Salt and black pepper to taste
1 tablespoon chopped fresh parsley *(optional)*

Cut and scrape the kernels from the corn and set them aside in a bowl.

Melt the butter in a skillet. Add the scallions (or shallots) and cook over low heat until softened, 3 to 4 minutes. Add the corn kernels along with the half-and-half, heavy cream, or crème fraîche. Cook, stirring as little as possible, over low heat until thickened, about 2 minutes. Season with salt and pepper to taste. Sprinkle parsley on top, if using. ◌

BAKED SQUASH WITH BUTTER
AND MAPLE SYRUP

....

SERVES 6 TO 8

—᠗ Many people associate squash with the holidays, and this dish may certainly be a part of any Thanksgiving or holiday celebration. It goes particularly well with mild meats such as turkey, pork, and roast chicken. However, I think this is an easy recipe to prepare any night, especially during the fall, when the days are getting shorter and we begin to crave comforting foods. It is a great alternative to mashed potatoes. Children love it, too.

6 pounds acorn or butternut squash, halved lengthwise and seeded
Salt and black pepper to taste
4 tablespoons (1/2 stick) unsalted butter
1/4 cup maple syrup

Preheat the oven to 400 degrees.

Place the squash, cut side down, on a baking sheet and bake for 45 minutes to 1 hour, until the squash is easily pierced with a fork. Scoop the flesh into a bowl and mash with a potato masher or a fork until fairly smooth. Season to taste with salt and pepper. Keep warm.

Combine the butter and maple syrup in a small saucepan and cook, stirring, over low heat until the butter is melted and blended with the syrup, about 2 minutes.

Stir half of the syrup mixture into the squash. Transfer the squash to a shallow serving dish. Pour the rest of the syrup mixture over the top.

NOTE: This may be prepared up to 2 days ahead. Cover and refrigerate. Reheat in a 350-degree oven for about 20 minutes. ᠗

FILLED GREEN PEPPERS

—⟳ Try making this dish in the summer, when the tomatoes are at their best. This dish is an easy, practical way to use up any green bell peppers you might have on hand in your refrigerator. It can be served cold on a picnic, and easily eaten by picking up each of the green bell pepper halves with your fingers, or it is just as good served hot on a plate at home.

2 tablespoons olive oil
2 green bell peppers, halved lengthwise, seeded,
    and ribs removed
3 cloves garlic, finely chopped
1 large onion, chopped
2 medium tomatoes, peeled and chopped
1 small eggplant, chopped
1 tablespoon chopped fresh oregano, or 1½ teaspoons crumbled
    dried oregano
Salt and black pepper to taste
Fresh basil leaves for garnish *(optional)*

Preheat the oven to 350 degrees. Lightly coat a 13 by 9-inch Pyrex baking dish with a little of the olive oil.

Put the green peppers into a pot of salted boiling water, place a plate in the pot on top of the peppers to keep them under the water, and parboil for 4 minutes. Remove and set aside. Heat the remaining olive oil in a sauté pan. Add the garlic and onion and cook over medium heat for a minute or two, just to soften them. Add the tomatoes, eggplant, oregano, and salt and pepper to taste. Stir to mix. Taste for salt and correct if necessary. Cover the pan and cook, stirring once or twice, over medium-low heat for 10 minutes. Uncover and cook, stirring often, for another 3 minutes. Remove from the heat.

Put the pepper halves, hollow side up, in the prepared baking dish. Using a slotted spoon, fill the halves with the tomato-and-eggplant mixture. Bake for 20 minutes. Remove and serve hot or cold, with fresh basil leaves on top if you like. ⌒

KEEPING
THE FLAME ALIVE

Men and women today are haunted by a sense that in the midst of plenty, our lives seem barren. We are hungry for a greater nourishment of the soul. In England today, a businessman-turned-philosopher, Charles Handy, has won a widespread following with his writing. Capitalism, he argues, delivers the means but not the point of life. Now that we are satisfying our outer needs, we must pay more attention to those within—for beauty, spiritual growth, and human connection.

—David Gergen,
U.S. News & World Report,
August 16–23, 1999

CANDIED CARROTS

⟶ Cooking times vary greatly with carrots, depending on their size and age.

1 pound carrots, peeled
Salt and black pepper to taste
6 tablespoons (3/4 stick) butter
1/4 cup packed light brown sugar

Slice or cube the carrots, or leave them whole if they are small. Cook them, covered, in 2 inches of boiling water until they are tender, about 10 to 12 minutes if they are sliced, longer if they are whole. Drain and season with salt and pepper to taste.

Melt the butter in a heavy skillet, stir in the brown sugar, and cook, stirring, until the sugar is melted. Add the seasoned carrots and cook slowly until they are well glazed. ⟶

SUGARED BEETS

⏤ℭ When buying beets, look for ones that still have their greens attached. Beet greens are delicious when chopped and sautéed with a little olive oil and salt. They can even be mixed in with the cooked beets to create a flavorful salad. As an alternative to boiling the beets, try wrapping them in foil and roasting them in a 450-degree oven until they can be pierced easily with a fork, 50 to 60 minutes.

1 pound beets
Butter
Salt
2 teaspoons sugar (or to taste)

Cut off all but 1 inch of the beet tops; do not pare or remove the roots. Drop the beets into enough boiling water to cover them, and cook, uncovered, until they are tender, allowing 30 minutes to 1 hour, depending on their size. Drain the beets, drop them in cold water for a minute or two to cool them slightly, and then slip off the skins. Slice them with an egg slicer or a knife. Toss them with butter and salt to taste, and the sugar. Reheat them if necessary before serving. ℭ⏤

RAINY DAY VEGETABLE COBBLER

⁓ There is nothing better than this vegetable cobbler served on a cold, rainy day. You won't be disappointed after making it.

VEGETABLES

1 turnip, peeled and cut into bite-sized wedges
1 russet potato, peeled and diced
1 celery root, peeled and diced
1 onion, coarsely chopped
3 carrots, peeled and sliced
1/2 cup chopped fresh parsley
1 cup chicken broth
1 tablespoon cornstarch
1 teaspoon salt
Black pepper to taste
4 tablespoons (1/2 stick) butter

DOUGH TOPPING

13/4 cups all-purpose flour
1 tablespoon baking powder
1/2 teaspoon salt
6 tablespoons (3/4 stick) cold butter, cut into pieces
3/4 cup heavy cream

Preheat the oven to 325 degrees.

To prepare the vegetables, put the turnip, potato, celery root, onion, carrots, and parsley in a 2-inch-deep, 3-quart baking dish (I use a 13 by 9 by 2-inch Pyrex baking dish). In a small mixing bowl, blend the chicken broth with the cornstarch. Pour over the vegetables and mix well. Add the salt and pepper to taste and mix to blend. Dot the top of the vegetables with the butter.

To make the dough topping, mix the flour, baking powder, and salt in a large mixing bowl, and stir with a fork to blend. Put the pieces of cold butter into the flour mixture and rub quickly with your fingertips until the dough resembles coarse crumbs. Using a fork, slowly stir in the cream until roughly mixed. Gather the dough into a shaggy mass and knead 5 or 6 times. Roll the dough out on a lightly floured surface until it is the size of the top of the baking dish. The dough topping should be about 1/4 inch thick. Place the dough on top of the vegetables.

Bake for 55 to 65 minutes, until the vegetables are cooked through and the crust is browned. Test the vegetables for doneness with a knife tip or skewer. Remove from the oven and serve hot. ⌀

SUCCOTASH

—☜ *Succotash* comes from the Narraganset Indian word *msíck-quatash,* meaning "boiled corn kernels." In any case, the end result is a very satisfying, tasty dish. Of course, it is always better to use fresh ingredients when available.

2 tablespoons butter
1 tablespoon all-purpose flour
2 cups frozen lima beans, cooked for 5 minutes
2 cups corn kernels (fresh if in season—*see Note for preparation*—or frozen)
1/4 cup water
1 teaspoon salt
1/4 teaspoon black pepper
1 teaspoon sugar
1/4 cup milk or cream

Melt the butter in a heavy saucepan; add the flour and cook, stirring constantly, for a minute or two. Add the lima beans, corn, water, salt, pepper, and sugar. Cook, stirring, over low heat for another minute, or until the mixture is thickened. Add the milk and heat thoroughly. Serve hot.

NOTE:

For fresh corn: If fresh corn is available, remove the husks and silk from 4 ears. Cut the stem off the large end of each cob, then stand the ear on a cutting board with the large, flat end down. Using a bread knife (a serrated blade is better for this job), cut down next to the cob so the kernels will fall off.

For frozen corn: Use one 10-ounce box each of frozen lima beans and frozen corn. Together they yield about 3 1/2 cups when cooked. To cook, bring a 3-quart (or smaller) pot of water to a boil. Dump both the corn and the limas into the boiling water. Cook for 1 minute, then bite into a lima bean; if tender, drain and proceed with the recipe. ✌

THE CENTER OF THE HOUSE

Cooking something delicious is really more satisfactory than painting pictures or making pottery. At least for most of us. Food has the tact to disappear, leaving room and opportunity for masterpieces to come. The mistakes don't hang on the walls or stand on shelves to reproach you forever. It follows from this that the kitchen should be thought of as the center of the house. It needs above all space for talking, playing, bringing up children, sewing, having a meal, reading, sitting, and thinking. . . . It's in this kind of place that good food has flourished. It's from this secure retreat that the exploration of man's curious relationship with food, beyond the point of nourishment, can start.

—Jane Grigson, *Good Things*

VEGETABLE BARLEY

⟿ Here is a wholesome and comforting dish when you are feeling like you need a little pick-me-up. It is a shame more people haven't learned to cook with barley. It is so good and nourishing.

2 tablespoons butter
1 large yellow onion, chopped
3 carrots, peeled, halved, and sliced
3 ribs celery, sliced
8 cups chicken broth
1 1/2 cups pearl barley
Salt and black pepper to taste
2 zucchini, sliced 1/4 inch thick
1 cup firmly packed fresh spinach leaves, washed

Melt the butter in a large soup pot and add the onion, carrots, and celery. Cook, stirring often, over medium heat for 5 minutes. Add the chicken broth, barley, and salt and pepper to taste. Simmer for 1 1/2 hours, or until the barley is tender, stirring every so often so the barley does not stick to the bottom of the pot.

Add the zucchini and spinach. Simmer for another 10 minutes. Taste and correct the seasoning. Serve hot. ⟿

BROCCOLI IN CHEESE CUSTARD

SERVES 6

‑‑‑ This custard recipe can also be used with other cooked vegetables, such as cauliflower, corn, onions, spinach, and cabbage.

2 cups cooked chopped broccoli
1/4 cup grated Cheddar cheese
3 eggs
1 1/2 cups milk or light cream
3/4 teaspoon salt
1/4 teaspoon black pepper

Preheat the oven to 350 degrees.

Butter a 1 1/2-quart baking dish, put the chopped broccoli in, and sprinkle with the cheese. Beat the eggs lightly in a bowl and stir in the milk, salt, and pepper. Stir into the broccoli-cheese mixture. Put the baking dish in a shallow pan and fill the pan with enough hot water to come halfway up the sides of the dish. Bake for 45 to 60 minutes, until the custard is set. ‑‑‑

COLCANNON

⟶ This is a wonderful and much-overlooked dish of Irish origin, made of cabbage and mashed potatoes.

2 pounds all-purpose potatoes, peeled and quartered
1 1/2 pounds green cabbage, quartered and cored
4 tablespoons (1/2 stick) butter
1 cup light cream or milk
1 teaspoon salt (or to taste)
Black pepper
6 scallions, thinly sliced

Put the potatoes in a large saucepan and add cold water just to cover. Bring to a boil and boil gently for 15 to 20 minutes, until tender when pierced with a fork. Halfway through the cooking, add the cabbage quarters. When the potatoes are tender, drain well. Remove the cabbage, slice into thin strips, and set aside. Return the potatoes to the pot. Add the butter, 1/2 cup of the cream, the salt, and the pepper to the pot with the potatoes and mash with a potato masher, fork, or electric mixer, smoothing out all the lumps. Add the remaining 1/2 cup cream, blending until you have a thick puree. Add the shredded cabbage and mix until well blended. Taste and correct the seasoning. Return the pot to low heat, stirring frequently until hot. Serve in a heated serving bowl garnished with the sliced scallions. ⟶

YESTERDAY'S SIDE DISH—
TODAY'S VEGETARIAN
CENTERPIECE

Spanish Rice

Pilaf

Fried Rice

Vegetable Frittata

Tomato Rarebit

Welsh Rabbit

Fresh Tomato Gratin Stew

Green Onion Pie

Yorkshire Pudding

Southern Corn Pudding

Crushed Macaroni and Vegetables

Zucchini Supper Dish

First-Prize Onion Casserole

Oregon Blue Cheese Crumble

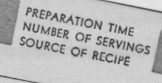

DISH

PREPARATION TIME
NUMBER OF SERVINGS
SOURCE OF RECIPE

Most of these dishes can be moved from the sidelines to center stage. As we Americans, particularly the young, are eating less and less meat, we are always on the lookout for satisfying nonmeat dishes. And the past is a great source, with all the vegetable dishes, casseroles, scallops, and rice dishes that were so prevalent in the old days.

SPANISH RICE

—~ Of course, I don't believe this dish is Spanish at all, but rather Cajun from Louisiana. I made it quite often in the 1960s. Then—as now—in home cooking, one had to watch the cost, and rice was an inexpensive way to fill out a meal; after all, rice feeds half the world. In most American homes at the time, rice was served buttered with salt and pepper. This recipe gave rice a little style, made it a delicious "fancy" side dish to serve alongside grilled meat or chicken. I always look forward to having any leftovers as a cold salad for lunch the next day. If you like a little added spice, put some hot pepper sauce on the table.

1/4 cup olive oil
2 onions, finely chopped
2 green bell peppers, seeded, ribs removed, and diced
2 ribs celery, finely chopped
3 cloves garlic, minced
1 cup long-grain white rice
One 8-ounce can tomato sauce
2 cups water
1 teaspoon salt
1/4 teaspoon black pepper
1 teaspoon cumin *(optional)*

Heat the olive oil in a large frying pan over medium heat, then add the onions, green peppers, and celery and sauté until soft, about 3 minutes. Add the garlic and cook for another minute while stirring. Add the rice and stir together to mix. Add the tomato sauce and the water carefully. Season with the salt and pepper, and add the cumin, if using. Bring to a boil, lower the heat, cover, and simmer for 20 to 25 minutes, until the rice is done, stirring once or twice. ~

PILAF

⟋ Pilaf is a seasoned rice dish common to many Eastern countries. It can be a whole meal made with fish, poultry, or meat, or a simple side dish made with herbs, spices, nuts, or raisins.

3 tablespoons olive oil
3 tablespoons finely chopped onion
1 cup long-grain rice
1/2 teaspoon salt
1/4 teaspoon black pepper
2 cups beef broth

Heat the olive oil in a saucepan over medium heat. Add the onion and cook, stirring often, until soft. Reduce the heat to low, add the rice, and cook, stirring constantly, for 3 minutes. Add the salt, pepper, and beef broth. Cover and simmer for 20 minutes, or transfer to a covered casserole and bake in a 350-degree oven for 1 hour.

MUSHROOM PILAF: Sauté 1 cup chopped mushrooms in 2 tablespoons butter, then combine with the broth before adding it to the rice mixture.

MEAT OR SEAFOOD PILAF: Add 1 cup chopped cooked chicken, beef, pork, or shrimp to the finished pilaf. (The meat should be thoroughly cooked.) It is a great way to use leftover meat from last night's supper. ⟋

FRIED RICE

—☙ Try adding diced cooked shrimp, pork, or chicken to the rice if you want to serve this as a supper dish.

1/4 cup vegetable oil
4 cups cooked rice
1/4 cup chopped green onions or scallions
1 1/2 tablespoons soy sauce
1/4 teaspoon black pepper
2 eggs, lightly beaten

Heat the oil in a large skillet and add the rice, green onions or scallions, soy sauce, and pepper. Cook, stirring often, over medium-high heat for 6 minutes. Add the eggs and stir briskly so they cook and break into small bits throughout the rice. As soon as the egg is set, remove the rice from the heat, and serve immediately. ☙—

VEGETABLE FRITTATA

—⌒ I am not usually keen on frittatas, as they are normally cooked too long and taste dry. This frittata is different. The pine nuts add a nutty sweetness and give character to this dish. I used to make this for Sunday dinner to serve with roast chicken. I would always double the recipe to make sure I had some left-overs. It is very good cold, and makes a fine lunch or supper served with a little salad and perhaps a slice of ham.

3 tablespoons olive oil
1 medium onion, chopped
1/2 cup pine nuts
2 large cloves garlic, minced
1 large (about 8 ounces) zucchini, sliced 1/4 inch thick
1 green bell pepper, seeded, ribs removed, and chopped
2 medium tomatoes, coarsely chopped (about 1 cup)
4 eggs
1 teaspoon salt
1/2 teaspoon black pepper
1 cup grated Monterey Jack cheese

Preheat the oven to 350 degrees. Grease an 11 by 7-inch Pyrex baking dish.

Put the olive oil in a large skillet and add the onion. Cook over medium-high heat until the onion is soft, about 3 minutes. Add the pine nuts and garlic, and cook for another minute. Add the zucchini, green pepper, and tomatoes, and cook, stirring often, until the vegetables are tender, 8 to 10 minutes.

Crack the eggs into a large bowl and beat them with the salt and pepper. Temper the eggs with some of the warm vegetables from the skillet by adding the vegetables a little at a time, stirring slowly to heat the eggs. Continue doing this until all the vegetables have been stirred into the eggs. You do not want to cook the eggs.

Put the vegetable-egg mixture into the baking dish and sprinkle the top evenly with the grated cheese. Bake for 15 to 20 minutes, until bubbles appear around the edges and the eggs are set and puffy. Serve immediately. ⌒

FAMILY STYLE EATING

"Family style" at its most basic dining table definition means that the food is put on platters and brought to the table, not portioned onto plates by the cook in the kitchen. But equally important as the substance—pasta, meatballs, chicken, all lifted easily from the platter—is the style, which emphasizes sharing, nurturing, and communication.

—Jeanne McManus, *Washington Post*

TOMATO RAREBIT

SERVES 4

——૭ This old-fashioned recipe can always be counted on to save the day or, rather, any supper. And what could be more comforting than spooning melted cheese over toast? You can make it in a pinch, as most of the ingredients are standard kitchen staples. And when fresh tomatoes aren't in season, good-quality canned tomatoes will do just fine.

2 medium tomatoes, finely chopped
1/4 teaspoon baking soda
2 tablespoons butter
2 tablespoons all-purpose flour
1 cup milk, heated
1 1/2 cups (5 ounces) grated Cheddar cheese
2 eggs
1 teaspoon dry mustard
1/4 teaspoon cayenne (or to taste)
Salt to taste
8 slices toast

Mix together the chopped tomatoes and the baking soda. Melt the butter in a saucepan, stir in the flour, and cook, stirring constantly, for 2 to 3 minutes. Slowly pour in the warm milk and stir until the mixture is smooth and thick.

Add the tomatoes and baking soda, cheese, eggs, mustard, cayenne, and salt to taste. Cook over very low heat, stirring, until the cheese has melted and the mixture is smooth and blended. Spoon over the toast and serve hot. ૭——

WELSH RABBIT

⟶☞ Known as both rabbit and rarebit in Wales and Scotland, here is another version of this tasty supper dish. This melted cheese dish should always be cooked gently, or the cheese will seize. This is ideal to be served in a grand old-fashioned chafing dish.

1/2 pound sharp Cheddar cheese, cut into small dice
1 tablespoon butter
1/2 teaspoon dry mustard
Cayenne to taste
1 egg, lightly beaten
Salt to taste
1/2 cup beer
4 slices toast

Mix together the cheese, butter, mustard, and cayenne in a heavy-bottomed pan, a chafing dish, or the top of a double boiler. Cook, stirring constantly, over low heat until the cheese has melted. Beat a little of the hot cheese mixture into the egg, and then return the egg-cheese mixture to the pan. Add salt to taste. Add the beer and cook for 1 to 2 minutes more, until the rabbit is very hot but not boiling. Spoon over the toast.

MILD RABBIT: Substitute 1/2 cup milk for the beer. ☞⟶

FRESH TOMATO GRATIN STEW

SERVES 6

—↷ This is one of the best recipes for tomatoes I have ever found. The results vary, depending on how juicy the tomatoes are. Sometimes the casserole is very soupy and is best served in small bowls; other times, the bread crumbs absorb most of the liquid and form a thick sauce. The more you make it, the more you will get a feel for it. No matter—this gratin is always delicious. Serve as a main dish at lunch or supper with a crunchy iceberg-lettuce salad and warm buttered crackers.

4 tablespoons (1/2 stick) butter
4 pounds tomatoes, cored and sliced about 1/2 inch thick
Coarse sea salt or kosher salt
Black pepper to taste
About 1 1/2 cups heavy cream
2 cups fresh bread crumbs *(see page 111)*
2 teaspoons chopped fresh thyme, or 1–1 1/2 teaspoons
    crumbled dried thyme

Preheat the oven to 375 degrees.

Grease the bottom and sides of an oval 2 1/2-quart baking dish with 1 tablespoon of the butter. Reserve another tablespoon of the butter. Place a layer of tomato slices in the bottom of the dish. Sprinkle with sea salt and pepper, and dot with some of the remaining 2 tablespoons butter. Make another layer of tomatoes, sprinkle with salt and pepper, and dot with butter. Continue the layers and seasonings until all the tomatoes are used. Press down firmly on the final layer. Sprinkle with salt and pepper, and dot with butter. Pour the cream over the tomatoes until it starts showing along the sides at the top.

Melt the reserved tablespoon of butter in a skillet. Stir in the bread crumbs and toss to coat with the butter. Stir in the thyme. Sprinkle the crumbs evenly over the top of the tomatoes. Season with salt and pepper. Bake for 45 minutes to 1 hour, until the top is nicely browned.

THE CORRUPTION OF TASTE

The flavor industry is highly secretive. Its leading companies will not divulge the precise formulas of flavor compounds or the identities of clients. The secrecy is deemed essential for protecting the reputation of beloved brands. The fast food chains, understandably, would like the public to believe that the flavors of their food somehow originate in their restaurant kitchens, not in distant factories run by other firms.

— Eric Schlosser, *Fast Food Nation*

GREEN ONION PIE

⟿ I used to make this in the spring when green onions were in season. But now you can find them (called scallions in the East) throughout the year in any market. You could add chopped ham or bacon, but I prefer the simple, delicate taste just the way it is. To scald cream or milk, pour it into a heavy saucepan and heat over medium-high until a ring of little bubbles appears around the edge of the pan. (Stand right there, because the cream can heat quite quickly and you don't want it to boil over.) Remove from the heat and you've done the job.

Basic Pastry Dough *(recipe follows)*
4 tablespoons (1/2 stick) butter
3 cups chopped green onions or scallions (tender white part
   with a little green)
2 cups cream, scalded
4 eggs, lightly beaten
Salt and black pepper to taste
1 tablespoon chopped fresh basil

Preheat the oven to 375 degrees.

Line a 9-inch pie pan with the rolled-out pastry dough. Pierce the dough all over the bottom with a fork, and line with aluminum foil. Bake for 15 minutes, or until lightly browned. Remove and set aside to cool a bit.

Melt the butter in a skillet and sauté the onions until soft and tender. Put the onions in the prebaked pie shell. Mix together the scalded cream and the eggs and pour over the onions. Season with salt and pepper to taste, and sprinkle with the basil. Bake in the preheated oven for 20 to 25 minutes, until a knife inserted near the center comes out clean. Serve immediately. ⟿

BASIC PASTRY DOUGH

MAKES ENOUGH FOR 1 SINGLE-CRUST
9-INCH PIE

⸺☙ Don't handle this pastry dough any more than necessary, or it will be tough; treat it firmly, not timidly, but don't fuss with it. The flour and shortening should not be blended too well; it is the bits of shortening left in the dough that puff and expand during baking and give the pastry its flaky texture. For that reason, the dough cannot be mixed as successfully in a food processor.

1½ cups all-purpose flour
¼ teaspoon salt
½ cup vegetable shortening
3 to 4 tablespoons cold water

Mix the flour and salt in a bowl. Cut in the shortening with a pastry blender or two knives. Mix lightly only until the mixture resembles coarse meal and some of the shortening remains the size of very tiny peas; the texture will not be uniform but will contain crumbs and small bits and pieces. Sprinkle the water over the flour mixture 1 tablespoon at a time and mix lightly with a fork, using only enough water so the dough will hold together. Press the dough together into a ball. If there are dry places that don't adhere, sprinkle a little more water over them. ☙⸺

YORKSHIRE PUDDING

—૭ First cousin to the popover, this crisp, golden-brown puff is a glorious accompaniment to roast beef dishes. Remove the roast from the oven 25 minutes before it is to be served. It's essential that the pudding be cooked in the roast beef fat and drippings, which flavor it so beautifully.

¼ cup roast beef pan drippings
2 eggs
1 cup milk
1 cup all-purpose flour
¾ teaspoon salt

Turn the hot oven up to 400 degrees and pour the pan drippings into a 9-inch square pan or an 11 by 7-inch pan. Put the pan in the oven to keep sizzling while you prepare the batter. Beat the eggs, milk, flour, and salt until well blended. Pour the batter into the prepared pan and bake for 25 to 30 minutes. Serve piping hot from the baking pan, giving a generous square with each helping of roast beef. ૭⌐

SOUTHERN CORN PUDDING

....

—◌ Although there is no better summertime treat than hot buttered corn on the cob, this delicate and genteel corn pudding is a close second. To free the corn kernels from the cob, use a trick the great Southern cook Edna Lewis shared with me. Cut the stem off the large end of the cob. Then stand the ear on a cutting board with the large, flat end down, and using a bread knife, cut down next to the cob so the kernels will fall off.

2 cups fresh corn kernels (from about 4 ears corn)
2 cups milk, heated
2 eggs, lightly beaten
2 tablespoons butter, melted
$1/2$ teaspoon salt
$1/8$ teaspoon black pepper

Preheat the oven to 350 degrees. Butter a $1^{1}/2$-quart casserole.

Mix all the ingredients together in a bowl. Pour into the casserole and place the casserole in a pan. Add enough hot water to the pan to come halfway up the sides of the dish. Bake for about 45 minutes, or until firm. ◌—

CRUSHED MACARONI
AND VEGETABLES

—☙ This recipe comes from a 6½ by 4½-inch paperback booklet with sixteen pages of recipes, printed in Lucca, Italy. I came across the recipe in my file and it sounded intriguing—you crush the macaroni with a rolling pin, sprinkle it over vegetables, top it with more vegetables and garlicky olive oil, and bake it for an hour. The result is a flavorful dish with bits of creamy macaroni tasting of olive oil and garlic. This is a winner!

¼ cup olive oil
⅓ cup water
3 large cloves garlic, finely chopped
1½ cups large macaroni, crushed with a rolling pin
3 tomatoes, cored and sliced ¼ inch thick
Salt and black pepper to taste
2 cups tightly packed stemmed fresh spinach leaves,
    well washed and cut into large pieces
½ cup finely chopped fresh parsley
1½ cups canned stewed tomatoes

Preheat the oven to 350 degrees. Grease an 8-inch square baking dish with 2 teaspoons of the olive oil.

Stir the remaining olive oil and the water in a small bowl to blend. Stir in the garlic.

Scatter the macaroni over half of a large dish towel and fold the other half of the towel so the macaroni is covered. Take a rolling pin and pound or roll it over the macaroni until the pasta is in small pieces.

Arrange the tomato slices in a single layer in the baking dish. Season generously with salt and pepper. Combine the spinach and parsley, and spread half of it over the tomatoes. Sprinkle the crushed macaroni over the top, and add a final layer of the spinach and parsley. Spread the stewed tomatoes over all of the ingredients. Drizzle the oil and garlic mixture evenly over the top. Cover the dish with aluminum foil and bake for 1 hour, or until the macaroni is tender. ᐓ

ZUCCHINI SUPPER DISH

⟶ Zucchini is one of the great pleasures of summer. I like to make this casserole using the homegrown zucchini that my friend's garden provides, but supermarkets are apt to have good zucchini year-round—just be sure it is firm.

1 pound zucchini (about 2 medium)
Salt
2 tablespoons unsalted butter
2 tablespoons vegetable oil
1 cup frozen corn, thawed (or fresh if in season)
1/3 cup canned mild green chilies, cut into strips
1 small onion, thinly sliced
2/3 cup heavy cream
Black pepper to taste

Cut the zucchini into 1/2-inch cubes. Toss it in a colander with 1 scant teaspoon salt and let "sweat" for 30 minutes. Pat the zucchini dry with paper towels.

In a large skillet, heat 1 tablespoon of the butter and 1 tablespoon of the oil over medium heat. When hot, add the zucchini and cook, stirring frequently, for 8 to 10 minutes, until lightly browned in spots. Using a slotted spoon, remove the zucchini from the skillet and transfer it to a shallow bowl.

Heat the remaining 1 tablespoon butter and 1 tablespoon oil in the skillet. When hot, add the corn, chilies, and onion, and cook, stirring frequently, over medium heat for 8 to 10 minutes, until the vegetables are mostly tender. Return the zucchini to the skillet and add the cream. Bring to a boil, then reduce the heat and simmer until the cream reduces and thickens slightly, about 5 minutes. Season generously with salt and pepper, and serve. ⟶

FIRST-PRIZE ONION
CASSEROLE

....

—꩜ Casseroles—food cooked and served in a casserole dish—with their complex flavors and textures, used to be very popular. They could be the perfect way to use up leftovers. This prize-winning casserole is still in my recipe box. It is delicious and a cinch to make. Sometimes I add a small can of green chilies to the dish. If I have any leftover casserole, I use spoonfuls of it as a filling for omelets.

5 cups water
Salt
1/2 cup long-grain white rice
4 tablespoons (1/2 stick) butter
4 large yellow onions, chopped into 1/2-inch pieces or smaller
6 ounces Swiss cheese, grated (a good full cup)
2/3 cup half and half or milk

Put the water in a saucepan and add 1 teaspoon salt. Bring to a boil, then slowly add the rice, reduce the heat, cover, and cook for just 5 minutes. Remove from the heat and transfer the rice to a large mixing bowl.

Melt the butter in a large sauté pan or skillet. Add the onions and cook, stirring, over medium heat until they are shiny and soft, 5 to 6 minutes. Put them into the bowl with the rice. Add the grated cheese and the half-and-half. Stir to mix all the ingredients well. Taste and correct the seasoning; you will probably need to add another 1/2 teaspoon or more of salt. Spread the rice mixture into a baking dish, and bake for 50 to 60 minutes, until lightly golden on top. ꩜

OREGON BLUE CHEESE
CRUMBLE

....

SERVES 8

⎯⟋ This recipe, a winner about twenty-five years ago in the
Mercer Island Reporter recipe contest, has become one of the
most popular hors d'oeuvres I serve. It's also delicious on grilled
steaks or hamburgers and as a topping for salads. Or serve the
crumble with sliced Granny Smith apples and wheat crackers as
the fruit-and-cheese course at dinner.

8 ounces blue cheese, crumbled (about 1 1/3 cup)
2 cloves garlic, minced
1/3 cup olive oil
2 tablespoons red wine vinegar
1 tablespoon lemon juice
1/2 cup chopped red onions (or chopped green onions)
1/2 cup minced fresh parsley
Black pepper to taste

Sprinkle the cheese into a shallow 6- to 8-inch dish. Mix together
the garlic and olive oil, and drizzle over the cheese. Combine the vinegar,
lemon juice, onions, and parsley, and pour over the cheese. Refrigerate
for 1 hour. Sprinkle pepper on top and serve. ⟍⟋

ONE-DISH MEALS
FOR SUPPER

Skillet Beans and Sausage

New England Boiled Dinner

Old-Fashioned Beef Stew

Meat Loaf

San Francisco Little Joe's

Ham Timbales

Beef Stroganoff

Irish Stew

Stuffed Cabbage Rolls

Shepherd's Pie

Chicken-Vinegar Sauté

Country Captain

Smothered Chicken with Mushrooms

Chicken Pie

Cod with Mustard Sauce

Skillet Fish Supper

Shrimp Crisp in Garlic Crumbs

Kedgeree

Salmon or Tuna Loaf

Cheese Fondue

Shirred Eggs

I'm calling this chapter "One-Dish Meals for Supper" because somehow that sounds simpler and more inviting—too many people are intimidated by the challenge of making a multiple-course "dinner" and having everything ready at the same time.

These supper recipes are essentially prepared in one dish or pan, although sometimes I have suggested easy accompaniments. Any of them can be served at lunch, too. But lunch, alas, is not a meal often eaten at home these days. However, any leftovers can be packed into a lunch box and taken to work or school; they'll taste much better than anything you can get at the cafeteria.

SKILLET BEANS AND SAUSAGE

—⌐ Easy to make and warming on a winter evening. Serve broccoli on the side and keep a jar of mustard handy.

1/4 cup olive oil
4 cloves garlic, chopped
1 medium onion, chopped
12 ounces kielbasa sausage, cut into 1/2-inch slices, then each slice quartered
Two 15-ounce cans cannellini beans, drained
2 tablespoons packed light brown sugar
1/2 cup white wine
1/4 cup red wine vinegar
1/4 cup chopped fresh parsley

Put the olive oil, garlic, and onion in a 12-inch skillet or 3-quart sauté pan and cook, stirring often, over medium-high heat for 3 to 4 minutes, until the onion is soft and starts to turn light brown. Add the cut-up sausage, beans, brown sugar, wine, and vinegar to the skillet. Simmer for 10 minutes, stirring often. Sprinkle the parsley on top and serve. ⌐2—

NEW ENGLAND BOILED DINNER

⁓ Serve this American classic with Mustard Sauce *(page 172)*, Horseradish Cream, Refrigerator Rolls *(page 46)*, and butter. Plan to have some leftovers for corned beef hash.

4 to 5 pounds corned beef brisket
4 medium onions, outer skins removed
6 medium potatoes, peeled
8 small beets
6 carrots, peeled
6 small turnips, scrubbed
1 medium head green cabbage, quartered and cored
Horseradish Cream *(recipe follows)*

Rinse the corned beef under cold running water to remove the brine. Place in a large pot, cover with cold water, and bring to a boil, skimming off the scum that rises to the surface during the first 10 minutes. Cover and simmer for 2 hours. Add the onions and potatoes, and continue to simmer. Meanwhile, bring a quantity of water to a boil in another saucepan and add the beets. Boil them for 30 to 40 minutes, until they are barely tender when pierced with a knife. Drain, place in an ovenproof serving dish, and put them in a 250-degree oven to keep warm. When the onions and potatoes have cooked for 15 minutes, add the carrots and turnips to the pot and simmer for 30 minutes more. Remove the meat, slice it, and arrange, surrounded by the vegetables, on an ovenproof platter. Place in the warm oven, with the beets. Bring the corned beef broth to a boil, and add the cabbage wedges. Boil for 3 minutes, drain, and place the cabbage in a separate serving bowl. Serve slices of beef with the accompanying vegetables and a spoonful of Horseradish Cream, if desired. ⌔

HORSERADISH CREAM

MAKES 1 GENEROUS CUP

3/4 cup heavy cream
1/4 cup prepared horseradish
2 tablespoons cider vinegar
Salt to taste

Beat the cream until stiff. Gently fold in the horseradish, vinegar, and salt. ∽

OLD-FASHIONED BEEF STEW

⏤⌐ A stew you will serve in soup bowls: dark brown beef and vegetables in lots of rich gravy.

1/3 cup all-purpose flour
1 teaspoon salt
1/4 teaspoon black pepper
2 pounds stewing beef
1/4 cup vegetable shortening
4 cups boiling water
1 tablespoon lemon juice
1 tablespoon Worcestershire sauce
1 teaspoon sugar
1 large onion, sliced
2 bay leaves
1/4 teaspoon ground allspice
12 small carrots, peeled and trimmed
12 small white onions
8 small new potatoes, peeled

Mix together the flour, salt, and pepper on a sheet of waxed paper and roll the beef cubes in the mixture. Shake off the excess. Melt the shortening over high heat in a Dutch oven or a heavy-bottomed pot with a cover. When the fat is very hot, add the beef, about 5 or 6 pieces at a time so as not to crowd them, brown on all sides, and remove. When the last batch of meat is a richly dark color, return all the pieces to the pot and pour on the boiling water. Stand back when you do so, because it will spit and sputter. Stir and add the lemon juice, Worcestershire sauce, sugar, onion, bay leaves, and allspice. Reduce the heat, cover, and simmer for 1 1/2 to 2 hours, until the meat is tender. Add the carrots, white onions, and potatoes, and cook for another 20 to 25 minutes, until they can easily be pierced with a fork. ⌐⌐

HOPE FOR THE FUTURE

We cannot ignore the meaning of mad cow. It is one more warning about unintended consequences, about human arrogance and the blind worship of science.

The same mindset that would add beef to your chicken nuggets would also feed pigs to cows. Whatever replaces the fast food industry should be regional, diverse, authentic, unpredictable, sustainable, profitable—and humble. It should know its limits. People can be fed without being fattened or deceived. This new century may bring an impatience with conformity, a refusal to be kept in the dark, less greed, more compassion, less speed, more common sense, a sense of humor about brand essences and loyalties, a view of food as more than just fuel. Things don't have to be the way they are. Despite all evidence to the contrary, I remain optimistic.

—Eric Schlosser, *Fast Food Nation*

MEAT LOAF

—∽ A hearty family meal, subject to many variations, meat loaf is great the second day served in sandwiches for lunch.

KETCHUP SAUCE TOPPING

3 tablespoons butter
One 6-ounce can tomato paste
1 teaspoon sugar
1/2 cup water
Salt and black pepper to taste

MEAT LOAF

2 cups fresh bread crumbs *(see Note)*
1 medium onion, chopped fine (1 1/2 cups)
2 eggs, lightly beaten
1 1/2 pounds ground beef
1 tablespoon Worcestershire sauce
1 tablespoon dry mustard
2 teaspoons salt
1/2 teaspoon black pepper
1/2 cup water

To make the topping, heat the butter in a saucepan. Whisk in the rest of the ingredients, and continue to whisk until the sauce is well blended and smooth. If the sauce becomes too thick, add a little more water. Makes 1 cup sauce.

To make the meat loaf, preheat the oven to 350 degrees. Butter an 11 by 4 1/2-inch baking dish.

Mix together all the meat loaf ingredients in a large bowl; your freshly washed hands are the best tools for the job. To check for proper seasoning, take out a small piece of the meat, cook it in a skillet, taste it, and adjust the salt and pepper. Place the meat in the baking dish and pat into a loaf shape; spread 1/2 cup ketchup sauce on top, brushing evenly *(see Note)*. Cover with aluminum foil and bake for 1 hour.

NOTE: To make fresh bread crumbs, tear the bread into pieces and place in a food processor or blender. Pulse until the crumbs are very fine.

The remaining ketchup sauce can be made into spaghetti sauce by adding your favorite fresh herbs or a little meat. ∽

....

SERVES 4

⤳ I made this dish a lot for my children when they were growing up; they never seemed to grow tired of it. It is good and wholesome, and simple to prepare.

3 tablespoons vegetable oil
1 onion, chopped
1 pound lean ground beef
1 pound fresh spinach, washed, blanched, and coarsely
    chopped (*see Note*)
Salt to taste
Tabasco
4 eggs, lightly beaten
1/4 cup grated Parmesan cheese

Heat the oil in a large skillet, add the onion, and cook over medium heat until the onion is soft. Add the beef, mixing with the onion and breaking it up into small bits with a fork; cook until the redness is gone. Add the spinach and mix well. Cook, stirring, for 3 to 4 minutes, then add salt to taste. Mix a dash or so of Tabasco with the eggs, then pour the eggs over the beef mixture and stir until they are set. Transfer to a warm platter and sprinkle with the Parmesan cheese.

NOTE: To blanch the spinach, drop it in a pot of rapidly boiling water for less than a minute. ⟲

HAM TIMBALES

‑꙰ A timbale is a cross between a custard and a soufflé, made in individual custard cups, or small molds, or even muffin tins; the timbales are then unmolded and served with a sauce. They may be made of almost any mixture of tasty cooked meat, poultry, fish, or shellfish, or vegetables and cheese, so they provide a good way of transforming leftovers into a delicious luncheon dish.

5 tablespoons butter
1/2 cup fresh bread crumbs
1 1/4 cups milk
2 cups minced ham
2 tablespoons minced fresh parsley
4 eggs, lightly beaten
Salt and black pepper to taste
Mustard Sauce *(page 172) (optional)*

Preheat the oven to 350 degrees. Using 1 tablespoon of the butter, lightly butter 8 custard cups or muffin tins.

Melt the remaining butter in a small saucepan, add the bread crumbs and milk, and cook, stirring occasionally, over medium-low heat for 5 minutes. Remove from the heat and stir in the ham, parsley, and eggs. Season to taste with salt and pepper. Fill the cups two-thirds full, place them in a pan, and fill the pan with enough hot water to come two-thirds of the way up the sides of the custard cups. Bake for 20 minutes.

Remove from the oven and let stand for 5 minutes, then unmold by slipping a knife around the inside of each cup and turning out onto a warm plate or a platter. Serve 2 per person, with hot Mustard Sauce or a sauce of your choosing. ꙰‑

BEEF STROGANOFF

....

—♋ Tender beef in a lightly tangy mushroom-flavored sauce spooned over toast makes for a delicious, simple meal. Named after a nineteenth-century Russian count, Beef Stroganoff was popular in this country during the 1960s and 1970s, and should be given another try. I think it is much better served over toast than over the rice or noodles usually called for.

2 pounds filet or tri-tip (triangle tip) of beef, cut into
    2 by ½-inch strips
Salt and black pepper to taste
2 tablespoons vegetable oil
2 large onions, chopped
¾ pound fresh mushrooms, wiped clean and sliced
2 cups beef broth
1½ cups sour cream
6 slices white bread, toasted

Sprinkle the meat with salt and pepper. Heat the vegetable oil in a large heavy-bottomed sauté pan, add the meat, and cook for just 1 minute over medium-high heat. Add the onions and cook, stirring often, over low heat for 4 to 5 minutes. Stir in the mushrooms, then the beef broth, and reduce the heat to a simmer. Simmer, stirring often, for 15 to 20 minutes, until the meat is tender. Taste and add more salt if needed.

Stir the sour cream briskly, then add to the beef mixture. Mix well, and allow the stroganoff to thoroughly heat through. Serve at once over the toast. ♋—

IRISH STEW

S E R V E S 4

~ Turnips, carrots, and onions are the foundation for this simple yet flavorful Irish lamb stew. Horseradish is a strong and welcomed accompaniment to the mild lamb.

3 pounds boneless shoulder of lamb
Salt and black pepper to taste
7 cups water
3 tablespoons vegetable shortening
4 medium carrots, peeled and cut into 1/4-inch pieces
2 white turnips, peeled and cut into 1/4-inch pieces
2 medium yellow onions, peeled and cut into 1/4-inch slices
2 bay leaves, torn in half
Prepared horseradish *(optional)*

Cut the meat into 1 1/2-inch cubes. Spread the meat on a piece of waxed paper and sprinkle the pieces liberally with salt and pepper. Set the meat aside. Bring the water to a boil. Melt the shortening over medium-high heat in a heavy pot or Dutch oven. Add the meat cubes and let them brown well on all sides. Add the boiling water to the meat pot. Stir and reduce the heat to medium-low; add the vegetables and the bay leaves. Stir again, cover, and cook for about 1 hour, or until the meat is thoroughly cooked and the vegetables are tender. Remove the bay leaves, taste, and add salt if necessary. Serve hot with horseradish on the side, if you wish. ~

STUFFED CABBAGE ROLLS

—☙ On a chilly night, there can't be a nicer supper than cabbage rolls with a little sour cream, warm homemade applesauce, and good rye crackers. Since it is simple to make twice as much, double the recipe and freeze the extra cabbage rolls for another night.

1 large head Savoy cabbage, halved and cored
3 tablespoons butter
1 medium onion, chopped (about 3/4 cup)
2 cloves garlic, finely chopped
2 cups tomato sauce
1/2 cup water
1 teaspoon ground allspice
Salt and black pepper to taste
1/4 cup packed light brown sugar
1 1/2 cups cooked white rice *(see Note)*
1 pound lean ground beef
Applesauce *(recipe follows)*
1 cup sour cream

Bring a large pot of salted water to a boil. Put the cabbage into the boiling water, cover, and let boil gently for 4 to 5 minutes. Drain well.

Melt the butter in a saucepan, add the onion and garlic, and cook, stirring, only until the onion is soft, not browned. Add the tomato sauce, water, allspice, and salt and pepper to taste. Reduce the heat and let the sauce simmer for about 15 minutes. Taste and correct the seasoning. The sauce should be thickened, but not so thick that it "plops" when poured from a spoon.

Gently remove the tough outer leaves from the cabbage and reserve. Remove 12 more leaves to make the rolls. Chop the remaining cabbage coarsely and spread over the bottom of a 13 by 9-inch oiled baking dish. Sprinkle the brown sugar over the chopped cabbage, then sprinkle lightly with salt and pepper.

Preheat the oven to 350 degrees.

Combine three-quarters of the sauce with the rice and beef, and mix well. Divide the filling into 12 approximately equal parts and spoon each portion onto a cabbage leaf. Starting from the stem end, roll up each leaf, tucking in the sides, and place the roll on the chopped cabbage, seam side down. Spoon a little of the remaining sauce on top of each roll. Cover the top with the reserved outer leaves. Bake for 1 hour in the pre-heated oven. Discard the topping of outer leaves and serve with sour cream and warm applesauce.

NOTE: To cook rice, use a deep, heavy-bottomed pot, bring 1 1/2 cups of water to a boil, and add 1/4 teaspoon of salt. Slowly stir in 1/2 cup of long-grained white rice so that the boiling does not stop. Cover, reduce the heat to low, and simmer for 20 minutes. Do not remove the lid during this time. After 20 minutes, all the water should be absorbed and the rice should be soft and fluffy. ᴖ

APPLESAUCE

MAKES 3 CUPS

ᴖ This is a recipe that really calls for your own taste judgment. If your apples are very tart, you won't need as much lemon juice as suggested here, and you may need more sugar. So taste, taste, taste.

4 large, firm, tasty apples, peeled, cored, and cut into
    eighths
1/2 cup water
Sugar to taste
3 tablespoons lemon juice

Put the apples and water into a sauté pan. Turn the heat to medium and cook, stirring often, until the apples become tender, 5 to 6 minutes. Add sugar to taste and the lemon juice, and stir to blend well. Cook for another 1 to 2 minutes. Remove from the heat and mash with a fork.

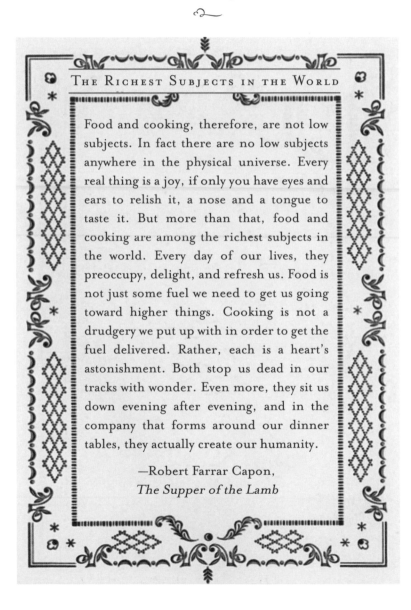

THE RICHEST SUBJECTS IN THE WORLD

Food and cooking, therefore, are not low subjects. In fact there are no low subjects anywhere in the physical universe. Every real thing is a joy, if only you have eyes and ears to relish it, a nose and a tongue to taste it. But more than that, food and cooking are among the richest subjects in the world. Every day of our lives, they preoccupy, delight, and refresh us. Food is not just some fuel we need to get us going toward higher things. Cooking is not a drudgery we put up with in order to get the fuel delivered. Rather, each is a heart's astonishment. Both stop us dead in our tracks with wonder. Even more, they sit us down evening after evening, and in the company that forms around our dinner tables, they actually create our humanity.

—Robert Farrar Capon,
The Supper of the Lamb

SHEPHERD'S PIE

—⌒ Shepherd's Pie was an ingenious way to use up Sunday's leftovers. For some, it was even more welcomed than the original roast.

3 cups roughly chopped cooked lamb
2 large cloves garlic, peeled
1 medium onion, quartered
1 teaspoon dried rosemary, crumbled
4 tablespoons (½ stick) butter
2 tablespoons all-purpose flour
¾ cup beef broth
Salt and black pepper to taste
4 medium potatoes, peeled, cooked, and mashed (about 3 cups)

Preheat the oven to 325 degrees.

Mix together the lamb, garlic, onion, and rosemary. Put through a meat grinder twice or chop in a food processor until fine. Melt the butter in a skillet and stir in the flour. Cook for a few minutes until smooth and blended. Slowly add the beef broth, whisking to avoid lumping. Cook, stirring, until the gravy is thickened, at least 5 minutes to get rid of the raw flour taste. Add the lamb mixture, stir to blend, and season with salt and pepper to taste. Spoon into a 1½-quart casserole or a deep pie pan. Spread the mashed potatoes on top and cover evenly to the edge of the casserole. Make a crisscross design with a fork. Bake for 45 to 50 minutes, until the meat is bubbling hot and the potatoes are browned. ⌒

CHICKEN-VINEGAR SAUTÉ

....

SERVES 4

—⌒ The simple addition of vinegar makes this a splendid dish. Vinegar and lemon juice both give the same sharp sparkle to many foods that are delicate in flavor.

One 2- to 3-pound frying chicken, in 8 pieces *(see page 121)*
Salt and black pepper to taste
6 tablespoons (3/4 stick) butter, or vegetable oil, or a combination
1/2 cup red wine vinegar
3/4 cup water
1 teaspoon minced garlic
1 tablespoon minced fresh tarragon, or 1 teaspoon dried
1 tablespoon minced fresh parsley

Sprinkle the chicken pieces with salt and pepper. Melt 4 tablespoons of the butter in a skillet over medium-high heat. Add the chicken, skin side down, and brown on all sides for 8 to 10 minutes. Pour 1/4 cup of the vinegar and all of the water over the chicken, cover the pan, and reduce the heat to low. Cook for about 15 minutes more, or until done. Remove the chicken to a serving dish and keep warm. Add the garlic to the skillet and cook for about 1 minute. Add the remaining 1/4 cup vinegar to the skillet and boil for another minute. Season to taste with salt and pepper, then add the remaining 2 tablespoons butter to the skillet and stir to blend. Pour the sauce over the chicken on the serving dish and sprinkle with the tarragon and parsley. Serve at once. ⌒

TO CUT UP A WHOLE CHICKEN:

1. Place the chicken, breast side down, on a nonporous work surface (not wood). Using a very sharp knife, cut through the backbone along the spinal column.
2. Turn the chicken over and break both sides of the breastbone by pushing down on it with the heel of your hand. Firmly flatten the chicken as much as possible.
3. Wiggle the wing joint at the shoulder, poking around with the tip of your knife until you feel the connecting tissue.
4. Cut through to remove the wing. Repeat with the other wing.
5. Wiggle the leg back and forth to see where it connects to the body. Pull down to help detect the connecting joint; when you find the socket, cut through it. Repeat with the other leg.
6. Cut each thigh from the drumstick at the joint.
7. Cut away the side of the breast, still attached to the back, severing the tiny bones. (Use the backbone for making stock.)
8. Cut the breast in half, starting just above the cartilage and probing with your knife to feel where the tissue gives way. Make the cut a little off center, where the bones are thin. The chicken is now in eight pieces, ready to be cooked.

COUNTRY CAPTAIN

....

SERVES 4 TO 6

—⌒ Cecily Brownstone, Associated Press's adroit columnist on things gastronomical, has made a thorough study of this dish, which has fascinated her over a period of time. She has constructed a version of it that was published in *Specialty of the House,* a cookbook compiled for the benefit of a local housing league. It's a delicious dish and one that you will want to make over and over again. Country Captain is as young today as it was a hundred years ago. Don't ignore this recipe.

One 2- to 3-pound frying chicken
1/4 cup all-purpose flour
1 teaspoon salt
1/4 teaspoon black pepper
4 tablespoons (1/2 stick) butter
2 tablespoons vegetable oil
1/3 cup finely diced onion
1/3 cup finely diced green bell pepper
2 cloves garlic, crushed
1 tablespoon curry powder
1/2 teaspoon crumbled dried thyme
One 16-ounce can stewed tomatoes, with liquid
3 tablespoons dried currants
Blanched toasted almonds

Have the chicken cut (or cut it yourself) into 8 pieces *(see page 121).* Wash the chicken pieces and pat them dry; coat with a mixture of the flour, salt, and pepper. Heat the butter and oil in a large skillet; brown the chicken on all sides. Remove the chicken and add the onion, green pepper, garlic, curry powder, and thyme to the skillet. Stir over low heat to loosen the browned particles. Add the stewed tomatoes. Return the chicken to the skillet, skin side up. Cover and cook slowly until tender, 20 to 30 minutes. Stir the currants into the sauce. Serve accompanied by almonds.

NOTE: After the chicken is browned and the sauce is made, the dish can be baked, covered, in a 325-degree oven for about 45 minutes, or until tender. Any leftover sauce would be delicious served over pasta.

BEST DONE OVER DINNER

Among virtually every culture on Earth, anything worth doing is best done over dinner. Bring out a nicely braised roast, a hot loaf of bread, and a slice of lemon pie, and rifts can be healed, pacts sealed, love revealed. Even the condemned do not want to leave the world without one last supper.

Natalie Angier,
New York Times, November 2000

SMOTHERED CHICKEN
WITH MUSHROOMS

⤳ The old-fashioned version of this dish called for heavy cream at the end of cooking. I have found the dish does not need the extra calories. This simple recipe tastes as good as it looks. A beginner cook should start with this.

One 3-pound frying chicken, in 8 pieces *(see page 121)*
Salt and black pepper to taste
1/4 cup olive or vegetable oil
1 1/2 cups chopped onions
1/4 cup all-purpose flour
2 cups chicken broth
1 pound fresh mushrooms, wiped clean and sliced
1/4 cup chopped fresh parsley

Preheat the oven to 400 degrees.

Season the chicken to taste with salt and pepper. In a large heavy-bottomed skillet, heat the oil over high heat and brown the chicken pieces, turning when necessary. Adjust the heat so that the chicken browns quickly but does not burn. Transfer the chicken to a shallow casserole large enough to hold the pieces in one layer. Add the onions to the skillet and cook, stirring frequently, for about 5 minutes, or until they are soft and lightly colored. Stir in the flour and mix it in well with a spoon. Pour in the chicken broth and, stirring constantly, bring to a boil. Reduce the heat and let the broth simmer for 2 to 3 minutes. Pour the sauce over the chicken in the casserole, cover tightly, and cook in the oven for about 20 minutes. Scatter the mushrooms over the chicken, re-cover, and bake for another 10 minutes, or until the chicken is tender. Sprinkle the parsley over the top and serve. ⤳

COOKED CHICKEN

When a recipe calls for cooked chicken, and you don't happen to have half a roast chicken in the refrigerator, buy a package of mixed parts, and arrange them, seasoned with salt and pepper, in one layer in a shallow baking pan. Bake them, covered loosely with aluminum foil, in a preheated 375-degree oven for 40 to 45 minutes. To test, cut into a thigh piece near the bone, and if the flesh is no longer pink, the chicken is done.

If a recipe calls for white meat only, buy chicken breasts. They will probably take only 30 minutes, but test in the same way to be sure.

CHICKEN PIE

—❦ This is a perfect dish for company. Everything can comfortably be made in advance and assembled quickly. A fresh fruit salad makes a fine companion for the chicken pie.

6 tablespoons (³/4 stick) butter
6 tablespoons all-purpose flour
2 cups chicken broth
1 cup heavy cream
¹/2 teaspoon black pepper
Salt
4 cups medium chunks of cooked chicken *(see page 125)*
12 small white onions, cooked
³/4 cup peas
³/4 cup diced peeled carrots
³/4 cup diced celery
Basic Pastry Dough *(page 95)*

Preheat the oven to 425 degrees.

Melt the butter in a saucepan, stir in the flour, and cook, stirring, for 2 minutes. Slowly add the broth, cream, pepper, and salt to taste. Cook for 5 minutes, until thickened and smooth. Put the chicken pieces in a deep pie pan or casserole, cover with the sauce, and stir in the onions, peas, carrots, and celery.

Roll out the prepared pie dough and place it over the casserole, allowing enough overhang so that the edges can be tucked under and crimped. Cut vents in the dough to allow the steam to escape. Bake for 25 to 30 minutes, until the crust is nicely browned. ❧

COD WITH MUSTARD SAUCE

SERVES 4

—ↄ This is a great recipe! Quick to assemble and cook, this cod dish is sharply flavored, and would be good served with buttered spinach and a pear-and-grape salad.

2 tablespoons olive oil
2 tablespoons Dijon mustard
1 tablespoon chopped fresh parsley
1/4 cup white vinegar
1/4 cup water
1/4 teaspoon salt
All-purpose flour
1 3/4 to 2 pounds cod fillets (or bass or red snapper)
Black pepper to taste
3 tablespoons butter or vegetable oil
Mustard Sauce *(page 172)*

Mix together the olive oil, Dijon mustard, parsley, vinegar, water, and salt in a small bowl, stirring well. Set aside.

Lightly flour the fish fillets and season with salt and pepper. Melt the butter in a skillet over medium-high heat and fry the fillets for 3 to 4 minutes on each side, until the fish is golden and flakes easily with a fork. When the fish is done, remove it to a serving dish and keep warm.

Pour the Mustard Sauce into the skillet and cook for only about 30 seconds, or until it is hot and bubbly. Pour over the fish or return the fish to the skillet and coat with the sauce. Serve at once. ↶

SKILLET FISH SUPPER

—ᴄ This is a fish chowder without the broth. To make this a perfect supper, cook spinach with lemon juice and a little grated lemon rind, and serve corn bread on the side. Skillet Fish Supper will become a frequent request. Use one or several kinds of fish.

5 tablespoons butter or vegetable oil
1 cup chopped onion
1½ cups diced peeled potatoes
1 cup corn kernels (from 2 ears corn)
1 pound fish fillets (cod, bass, snapper, or halibut), cut into
    1-inch chunks
Salt and black pepper to taste
⅓ cup chopped fresh parsley

Heat 4 tablespoons of the butter or vegetable oil in a large skillet over medium-high heat, then add the onion and potatoes and cook slowly until the potatoes are tender. Stir in the corn kernels and the remaining 1 tablespoon butter. Add the fish chunks and salt and pepper to taste, and continue cooking, stirring occasionally, until the fish is cooked through, about 5 minutes. Be careful not to break up the fish while stirring. Sprinkle with the parsley and serve. ᴄ

SHRIMP CRISP IN
GARLIC CRUMBS

....

⎯☙ Serve with ripe tomatoes and a nice green salad.

4 slices bread (sourdough bread preferably)
6 large cloves garlic, sprinkled with salt and then chopped
3/4 cup olive oil
8 ounces cooked shrimp *(see page 143)*
2 tablespoons finely chopped fresh parsley
Salt and black pepper to taste
3 eggs
1/2 lemon

Preheat the oven to 350 degrees.

Trim the crusts from the bread and discard. Tear the slices into pieces and whirl in a food processor to make 3 cups of fine crumbs. In a large, shallow casserole, heat the garlic in the olive oil in the oven for about 10 minutes, or until the oil bubbles a little and the garlic begins to cook. Remove from the oven.

Mix the bread crumbs with the oil and garlic in the casserole. Put back in the oven and bake until the crumbs are crisp and golden, about 20 minutes, stirring after 10 minutes so they bake evenly. Remove from the oven and add the shrimp, parsley, and a generous amount of salt and pepper. Break the eggs over the top and stir just to mix. Squeeze the 1/2 lemon over the top, stir once more, and put back in the oven to bake for another 5 to 10 minutes. ☙

KEDGEREE

⟶ In the eighteenth century, Kedgeree was very popular as an Indian breakfast dish. It was embraced by the English and later by Americans, and it has been served as a supper dish. Its popularity was enormous for many, many years. Kedgeree is too good to be a lost recipe. It is easy to make, particularly if you have some leftover cooked fish.

2 tablespoons butter or vegetable oil
2 tablespoons finely chopped onion
1/4 to 1/3 cup finely chopped green bell pepper
1/2 teaspoon curry powder (or more to taste)
1/2 teaspoon summer savory
2 cups cooked rice *(see page 117)*
2 cups flaked cooked fish, such as sole or cod fillets *(see Note)*
Salt and black pepper to taste
1/2 cup milk

Heat the butter or oil in a large skillet and quickly cook the onion and green pepper over medium heat, without browning them. Stir in the curry powder, savory, cooked rice, and flaked fish, mixing thoroughly. Add salt and pepper to taste and a little more curry, if desired. Stir in the milk and bring the mixture to the boiling point. Serve immediately.

NOTE: To cook and flake fish, heat 1 to 2 tablespoons of vegetable oil in a sauté pan and add the fish. Cook for 1 to 2 minutes on each side, until the fish is opaque. Remove from the pan and use a fork to break up the fish into flakes. ⟶

SALMON OR TUNA LOAF

....

SERVES 6

—∽ This is a winner! And it's made from ingredients you're apt to have right in the cupboard. You can serve it hot or cold and it is equally good. If you serve it cold, you won't need the sauce; try it instead with the Cold Asparagus with Sesame Mayonnaise *(page 63)*.

2 cups cooked or well-drained canned salmon or tuna
1/2 cup fresh bread crumbs
4 tablespoons (1/2 stick) butter, melted
2 eggs, well beaten
1 1/2 tablespoons minced onion
2 teaspoons minced fresh parsley
1 tablespoon minced green bell pepper
1/4 teaspoon Worcestershire sauce
Dash of Tabasco
Salt to taste
Mustard Sauce *(page 172)*

Preheat the oven to 350 degrees. Butter a 1-quart loaf pan.

Mix together the fish, bread crumbs, melted butter, eggs, onion, parsley, green pepper, Worcestershire sauce, Tabasco, and salt. Press into the loaf pan, and bake for about 35 minutes. Serve with the Mustard Sauce. ∽

CHEESE FONDUE

—৯ During the late sixties and early seventies, nearly everyone owned a fondue pot and used it. One of the appeals of eating this Swiss classic was the primal act of sitting around the fondue pot, spearing chunks of bread on long forks, and dunking the bread into the hot, creamy cheese sauce. Originally, Swiss fondue was a frugal dish the Swiss conceived to use up stale bread and old hard cheese. When we got wind of fondue, we turned it into the trendiest fad ever. Give fondue another try; it is good fun and worth making. Try cutting up your favorite vegetables and dunking them in the hot cheese sauce along with the bread. You won't end up with any leftovers to worry about with this dish.

12 ounces Gruyère or Emmentaler cheese, grated (3 cups)
2 tablespoons all-purpose flour
2 cloves garlic, peeled
1¾ cups dry white wine
Salt and white pepper to taste
Ground nutmeg to taste
2 tablespoons butter
⅓ cup heavy cream
French bread, trimmed of crust and cut into small cubes

Mix together the grated cheese and the flour.

Boil the garlic and wine together until the wine is reduced to three-quarters of the original amount. Strain into a 1½-quart earthenware casserole. Discard the garlic. Place the casserole over hot (not boiling) water. Add ¼ cup of cheese at a time, stirring until each addition is completely mixed with the wine before adding another. When all the cheese has been blended in, add salt, white pepper, and nutmeg to taste. Add the butter and cream, and mix well.

To serve, place the casserole on an electric warmer (or place the fondue in a chafing dish) on the dining table. Spear each cube of bread with a fork and dunk in the fondue with a stirring motion. If the fondue becomes too thick, stir in a little more warm wine or cream.

SHIRRED EGGS

⟿ We should never have forgotten about shirred eggs. They couldn't be easier to prepare and they are pleasing to everyone. Recipes in the old days always called for cooking them in ramekins, but today, I'm afraid, no one knows what a ramekin is, much less has one. A ramekin is a shallow cuplike container that is heatproof. You may use instead any small Pyrex container that comfortably holds an egg. Muffin tins are a good answer if you are serving many. I think one has to plan on two eggs per person. They are particularly delicious baked with some cooked, crumbled bacon or bits of ham scattered over the bottom of the cup with the egg on top, then topped with grated cheese.

4 tablespoons (½ stick) or more butter, softened
12 eggs
Salt and black pepper to taste
About ⅓ cup grated sharp Cheddar cheese

Preheat the oven to 325 degrees.

Melt the butter in a small pan. Put 1 teaspoon or more (it doesn't hurt to be generous with the butter) into each small baking cup and swirl it around to coat the bottom and sides. Crack each one of the eggs into a buttered cup, then sprinkle lightly with salt and pepper.

Bake for 6 minutes, or until the eggs are almost set. Quickly sprinkle on the grated cheese and bake another 2 to 3 minutes. Tip and tilt a cup, and if the egg white has lost its translucence and looks set, the egg is done. With a small spoon, remove the eggs gently from the cups onto 6 warm plates, serving 2 per person. ⟿

REAL SALADS
AND DANDY DRESSINGS

Brown Derby Cobb Salad

Carrot Slaw

Coleslaw with Boiled Dressing

Shrimp Rémoulade

Wedges of Iceberg with White Cheddar
and Chive Dressing

Potato Salad

Waldorf Salad

Chicken, Fruit, and Curry Salad

Tomato Aspic

Cucumber Aspic

Spinach, Mushroom, and Bacon Salad

Salade Niçoise

Celery Victor

Crab or Shrimp Louie

Poppy Seed Dressing

Very Good Salad Dressing

Green Goddess Dressing

In these days when almost every salad we're served is made up of baby greens dressed—and often drowned—in a sharp vinaigrette, it is refreshing to turn to some early treasures. There used to be more variety in salad dressings, many of them sweetened and often thickened with flour and/or egg yolks and cream, and maybe perked up with a little curry or poppy seed. Many of those earlier salads were substantial enough to make a full lunch or a summer supper.

The aspics (before Jell-O gave aspic such a bad rap) are lightly jelled and full of natural flavors that I think you'll enjoy. They also look so attractive on the table with all their layers and colors.

BROWN DERBY COBB SALAD

—⌒ Whenever I see Cobb Salad on a menu, I have to order it. It has so many of my favorite ingredients—bacon, Roquefort cheese, and ripe avocados. Try making this for your next luncheon and your guests will be asking for the recipe.

1/2 large head lettuce, shredded
2 chicken breasts, cooked *(see page 125)*, chilled, and diced
2 medium tomatoes, diced
3 hard-boiled eggs, chopped
6 slices bacon, fried crisp and crumbled
3/4 cup (3 ounces) crumbled Roquefort cheese
2 medium avocados, halved, peeled, and cut into wedges
1 small head Belgian endive, leaves separated
1 tablespoon chopped fresh chives *(optional)*
1/2 cup Brown Derby French Dressing *(recipe follows)*

Place the shredded lettuce in a large bowl. Over the lettuce, arrange a row each of chicken, tomatoes, eggs, bacon, and cheese. Tuck in the avocado wedges and endive leaves to garnish. Sprinkle all with the chives, if desired. Toss at the table with the 1/2 cup dressing; if this seems a little sparse, taste and add more, a little at a time, until all the ingredients are well coated. ⌒—

BROWN DERBY FRENCH DRESSING

MAKES 3 CUPS

1/2 cup red wine vinegar
1/2 cup water
1 tablespoon lemon juice
1 1/2 teaspoons black pepper
1 teaspoon salt
1/2 teaspoon sugar
1/2 teaspoon dry mustard
1 1/2 teaspoons Worcestershire sauce
1 clove garlic, minced
1 1/2 cups vegetable oil
1/2 cup olive oil

Put all the ingredients except the oils in a jar, then screw on the lid and shake to blend. Add the oils and re-cover; shake vigorously to mix well. Chill thoroughly; shake again before using. The dressing will keep up to 5 days refrigerated. ᴓ

CARROT SLAW

⁓ A great old favorite that children particularly love.

6 medium carrots, peeled
3/4 cup diced celery
1/4 cup diced onion
1/3 cup raisins
1/2 cup diced unpeeled apple
1/2 cup mayonnaise
Salt and black pepper to taste

Grate the carrots by hand or in a food processor. Toss with the celery, onion, raisins, and apple. Mix in the mayonnaise, season well with salt and pepper, and chill thoroughly. ⌒

WISHING YOU A VERY HAPPY NEW YEAR

WEIGHTY PROBLEM: WHAT SHOULD PARENTS DO?

Childhood obesity is a family issue, and we shouldn't just target the child. Improving the eating habits and activity levels of the entire family is necessary. Limiting TV viewing, video games, and computer time is essential. Physical activity is also important. I truly believe that unless a child learns to enjoy vegetables, fruits, whole-grain foods, and physical activity, little can be done.

—Dr. Richard Strauss, in *People*, February 19, 2001

THE MEANING OF NOURISHMENT

Family food in Italy—or anywhere—is not about sustenance, but about nourishment, comfort, and togetherness, that you were taken care of at the end of the long day.

—Micol Negrin,
Rustico: Regional Italian Country Cooking

COLESLAW
WITH BOILED DRESSING

....

SERVES 4

—◌ I challenge you to find another coleslaw recipe this simple and good. A tangy dressing, shredded cabbage, and crunchy celery seed—it's all you need to make this classic summer dish.

BOILED DRESSING

1½ tablespoons all-purpose flour
1 teaspoon dry mustard
1 tablespoon sugar
2 egg yolks, lightly beaten
Pinch of cayenne
1½ tablespoons butter, melted
¾ cup milk
¼ cup cider vinegar
Salt to taste

COLESLAW

1 medium head green cabbage
1 teaspoon celery seed
Salt to taste

To make the boiled dressing, mix the flour, mustard, and sugar together in a heavy-bottomed pan. Slowly add the egg yolks, cayenne, melted butter, milk, and vinegar. Cook, stirring constantly, over low heat until thickened and smooth. Add salt to taste. Remove and store covered in the refrigerator until needed.

To make the coleslaw, cut the head of cabbage in half, place in a bowl of cold water, and refrigerate for 1 hour. Drain well. Shred finely, and add the dressing and celery seed. Toss to mix well and add salt to taste.

◌

SHRIMP RÉMOULADE

⎯☙ Rémoulade is a classic sauce that can be served with many things—fish, artichokes, and seafood, to name a few. However, I still think it's best served with shrimp.

1½ pounds shrimp

DRESSING

1 cup mayonnaise
2 cloves garlic, finely minced
1 small onion, finely minced
1 hard-boiled egg, finely chopped
1 dill pickle, finely minced
4 sprigs fresh parsley, finely minced
1 teaspoon dried tarragon
1 teaspoon dry mustard
1 teaspoon black pepper

Cook the shrimp *(see page 143)* and chill.

Mix the mayonnaise, garlic, onion, hard-boiled egg, dill pickle, and parsley together in a bowl. Season with the tarragon, dry mustard, and pepper. Mix well and let stand 1 hour before using.

Serve on small plates with Boston lettuce on the bottom, rémoulade sauce piled in a small mound in the center, and the shrimp arranged around the sauce. ☙

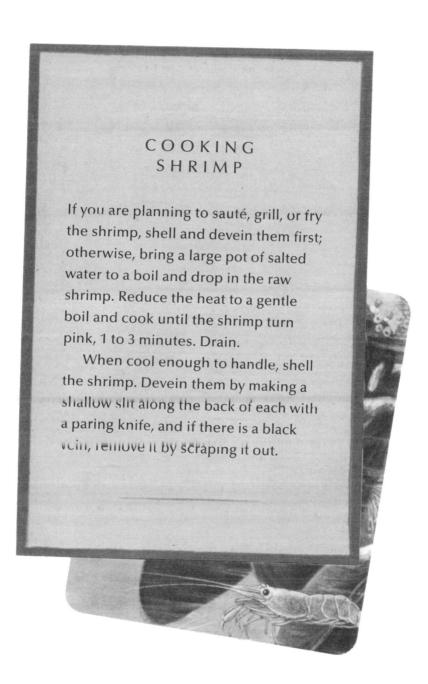

COOKING
SHRIMP

If you are planning to sauté, grill, or fry the shrimp, shell and devein them first; otherwise, bring a large pot of salted water to a boil and drop in the raw shrimp. Reduce the heat to a gentle boil and cook until the shrimp turn pink, 1 to 3 minutes. Drain.

When cool enough to handle, shell the shrimp. Devein them by making a shallow slit along the back of each with a paring knife, and if there is a black vein, remove it by scraping it out.

WEDGES OF ICEBERG WITH WHITE CHEDDAR AND CHIVE DRESSING

....

SERVES 6

—๑ Move over, radicchio, make room for the iceberg. I don't care what anyone says about this poor underappreciated and maligned lettuce; it wins my vote every time for its wonderful crispness and sturdiness. No soggy mess with this lettuce, and there is nothing better when it is served ice cold on a summer's day.

1 cup olive oil
2 teaspoons white wine vinegar
2 tablespoons lemon juice
4 ounces aged white Cheddar cheese, broken into 5 or 6 pieces
1/4 cup sour cream
1 teaspoon salt
Black pepper to taste
5 or 6 fresh chives
10 to 12 fresh basil leaves, plus 6 small fresh basil sprigs
6 generous wedges of iceberg lettuce
18 small golden or red tomatoes, cut in half

Place the olive oil, vinegar, lemon juice, cheese, sour cream, salt, pepper, chives, and basil leaves in a blender or food processor and blend briefly until well mixed and the herbs are chopped. Do not overmix—the dressing should retain some lumps of Cheddar. Correct the seasoning with salt and pepper. If you wish thinner dressing, add a small amount of water. Serve over the wedges of lettuce and garnish with the tomatoes and basil sprigs. ๑๏

POTATO SALAD

⟶ Potato Salad makes a wonderful supper served with lots of hard-boiled eggs and a platter of lettuce and tomatoes. The secret to making this good potato salad is to toss the potatoes while they are still hot with the lemon juice and oil.

2 pounds red or white new potatoes, scrubbed
1/4 cup olive oil
1/4 cup lemon juice
3 ribs celery, diced
About 11/4 cups mayonnaise
Salt and black pepper to taste

Boil the unpeeled potatoes until barely tender, about 15 minutes. They are done when they are easily pierced with a fork. (Potatoes continue to cook after they have been removed from the heat.) Drain, and as soon as they are cool enough to handle, peel and cut into 1/2-inch cubes.

While the potatoes are still hot, put them in a large mixing bowl, sprinkle with the oil and lemon juice, and toss until the cubes are completely coated. Add the celery and mayonnaise. Season with salt and pepper to taste and toss until well distributed. Serve chilled or at room temperature.

NOTE: This salad needs enough salt, pepper, and lemon juice to give good balance. Be generous enough with the mayonnaise so the salad is moist. ⟶

WALDORF SALAD

⎯↷ Waldorf Salad harks back to the tearoom, where it was served with tiny crustless white chicken sandwiches. This recipe is quite generous with the walnuts and celery, and the addition of applesauce makes a superior dressing.

DRESSING

1/2 cup mayonnaise
1/2 cup applesauce
3 tablespoons honey
1 tablespoon lemon juice

SALAD

3 or 4 crisp, firm green apples (Pippins or Granny Smiths)
2 or 3 ribs celery
1 1/2 cups walnuts, in large pieces
Salt to taste
Butterhead or iceberg lettuce leaves

To make the dressing, mix together the mayonnaise, applesauce, honey, and lemon juice in a small bowl.

To make the salad, core the unpeeled apples and cut them into bite-sized chunks. Chop the celery into 1/2-inch chunks. Put the apples, celery, and walnuts in a large bowl and sprinkle lightly with salt. Pour the dressing over, mix well, and serve on a bed of lettuce leaves. ↶

CHICKEN, FRUIT, AND CURRY SALAD

....

⎯⌒ This chicken salad recipe should never be forgotten. With its chunks of pineapple and crunchy pieces of water chestnut, and the surprise flavoring of curry, it is delicious from the first bite and people will ooh and aah. The salad can be served on top of butterhead lettuce leaves or sandwiched between two pieces of whole wheat bread.

SALAD

4 cups diced cooked chicken *(see page 125)*
2 cups grated coconut
One 5¹/₂-ounce can pineapple chunks, cut in half
2 cups halved grapes (seeds removed if necessary)
1 cup sliced water chestnuts
1 small can cashews *(optional)*
1 small can smoked almonds, cut in half

DRESSING

1¹/₂ cups mayonnaise
1 teaspoon curry powder (or more to taste)
1 tablespoon lemon juice
1 tablespoon soy sauce

To make the salad, put the chicken, coconut, pineapple chunks, grapes, and water chestnuts in a large bowl. Toss to mix well.

To make the dressing, mix together the mayonnaise, curry powder, lemon juice, and soy sauce in a small bowl and stir until well blended.

Just before serving, stir the dressing into the salad to blend evenly. Add the cashews, if using them, and the almonds, and mix. ⌒⌒

TOMATO ASPIC

....

SERVES 6

—᷉ Tomato Aspic is good with so many things—cold seafood and chicken, and other cold meats, or just by itself on a bed of lettuce with a dollop of good homemade mayonnaise on top. Try this as a luncheon dish served with deviled eggs, black olives, and Ice-Water Crackers *(page 43)*.

2 envelopes gelatin
1/3 cup water
4 cups tomato juice
1 onion, sliced thin
1/4 cup chopped celery leaves
2 1/2 teaspoons sugar
1 teaspoon salt
1/2 teaspoon black pepper
1 tablespoon pickling spice
1/4 cup lemon juice

Sprinkle the gelatin into a small bowl, add the water, stir, and let stand. Combine the tomato juice, onion, celery leaves, sugar, salt, pepper, and pickling spice in a saucepan. Bring to a boil, reduce the heat, and simmer for 5 minutes. Remove from the heat, strain, and stir in the softened gelatin, continuing to stir until the liquid clears. Add the lemon juice. Pour into a 1-quart mold *(see Note)* or a glass bowl and chill until set, 2 to 6 hours, or overnight to be safe. Unmold or simply spoon from the bowl to serve.

NOTE: If you plan to unmold the aspic, pour the gelatin mixture into a clean mold that has been rinsed but not dried, cover the top with aluminum foil, and chill. When the aspic is set, dip the outside of the mold into hot water for a few seconds (be careful not to let the top get wet).

Remove the foil, place a serving platter upside down on top of the mold, and invert so the salad is upright on the platter.

TOMATO ASPIC WITH VEGETABLES: Fill the bottom ½ inch of a 1-quart mold with some of the gelatin mixture before adding the lemon juice; chill until just set. Toss 1½ cups finely diced raw vegetables, such as celery, zucchini, cucumber, or red and green peppers, with the lemon juice and distribute over the aspic. Add the remaining gelatin and chill until ready to unmold and serve.

TOMATO ASPIC WITH SHRIMP: Fill the bottom ½ inch of a 1-quart mold with some of the gelatin mixture; chill until barely set. Distribute small cooked shrimp *(see page 143)* in a decorative pattern over the aspic, then spoon more of the gelatin mixture over and around the shrimp and chill. When set, add the remaining gelatin and refrigerate until ready to unmold and serve. ✑

CUCUMBER ASPIC

⟶ This is wonderful with cold salmon or chicken and deviled eggs.

1 envelope plus 1 teaspoon gelatin
1/2 cup cold water
2 1/2 cups chicken broth
1/4 cup grated onion
3 cucumbers, peeled, seeded, and grated *(see Note)*
Juice of 1 lemon

In a small bowl, stir the gelatin into the water and let stand for 5 minutes. Heat the chicken broth to a simmer, remove from the heat, and stir in the softened gelatin until it has completely dissolved. Let the gelatin mixture cool. Stir in the onion, cucumbers, and lemon juice. Pour into a square dish and chill for at least 4 hours, until set. Cut into squares to serve.

NOTE: To seed a cucumber, cut it in half lengthwise. Using a teaspoon, scrape out the seeds and discard them. ⟶

SPINACH, MUSHROOM, AND BACON SALAD

—⌒ This was a novelty first popular in the fifties. Before that no one had ever heard of using raw spinach in a salad. Spinach has since lost its popularity in salads to more trendy greens, but this combination is still the best—young, tangy spinach, salty bacon, and the slight muskiness of raw mushrooms.

1 pound fresh young spinach
4 ounces fresh mushrooms, wiped clean and thinly sliced
2 hard-boiled eggs, coarsely chopped
1/2 cup vegetable oil
1/2 teaspoon toasted sesame oil *(optional)*
1 teaspoon sugar
3 tablespoons lemon juice
1/2 teaspoon Dijon mustard
Salt and black pepper to taste
5 slices bacon, fried crisp and crumbled

Wash and dry the spinach and discard the stems. If the leaves are small, leave whole; if large, cut or tear them into bite-sized pieces. Toss the spinach, mushrooms, and eggs together in a salad bowl. Mix together in a separate bowl the vegetable oil, sesame oil, if using, sugar, lemon juice, mustard, and salt and pepper to taste. Beat well, then pour over the salad and toss until all the spinach leaves are coated. Serve on individual plates and sprinkle the bacon over each serving. ⌒

SALADE NIÇOISE

—↢ Full of the flavors of the Mediterranean, "Niçoise" refers to the use of peppers and olives in this salad. There are many variations of this recipe floating around, but this is one of the most authentic I've seen.

1 small head lettuce
1 cup lightly cooked green beans (boil for 5 minutes, then run
    under cold water to stop the cooking)
1½ cups cubed cooked new potatoes *(see page 145)*
One 6-ounce can tuna, drained
French Dressing *(recipe follows)*, made with the 1 teaspoon minced
    garlic
4 anchovy fillets
8 black olives
½ green bell pepper, in thin strips
2 hard-boiled eggs, quartered

Tear up the lettuce and mix it with the green beans and new potatoes in a salad bowl. Drain and break up the tuna, and add it to the salad with all but a couple of tablespoons of the dressing. Toss everything together. Arrange the anchovy fillets, olives, green pepper strips, and eggs decoratively on top of the salad and drizzle with the remaining dressing. ↢

FRENCH DRESSING

SERVES 4

2 tablespoons red wine vinegar (or more to taste)
1/2 teaspoon salt
1 teaspoon minced garlic *(optional)*
1/4 teaspoon black pepper
1/2 cup olive or vegetable oil

Mix the vinegar and salt together in a small bowl and let stand for a few minutes. Add the garlic, if using, and the pepper, and slowly stir or whisk in the oil. Taste for acid and salt and add more if too bland. Stir to blend before using, or store in a jar with a tight lid and refrigerate. Shake well before using. ❧

CELERY VICTOR

SERVES 6

—⌒ Victor Hirtzler, *chef de cuisine* at San Francisco's elegant
St. Francis Hotel, first introduced this winning salad in 1919.
This is as great today as it was more than eighty years ago.

3 bunches celery
About 1½ cups chicken broth
Herb bouquet of 1 bay leaf, 4 fresh parsley sprigs, and
    celery leaves (tied together)
Salt and black pepper to taste
3 tablespoons tarragon vinegar
½ cup olive oil
Celery leaves, for garnish

Trim the celery bunches, cutting off the outer ribs (save them for
soup), and cut each bunch in half lengthwise. (Set aside some celery
leaves for the herb bouquet and a few more for garnish.) Arrange in a
large saucepan and pour in enough chicken broth to barely cover the celery. Add the herb bouquet and salt and pepper to taste, and cook until
the celery is barely tender, about 6 minutes. Let the celery cool in the
broth, then remove the herb bouquet. Beat the vinegar into the olive oil.
Drain the celery, pour the vinegar-and-oil mixture over, and chill. Serve
garnished with celery leaves.

CELERY VICTOR WITH MUSTARD MAYONNAISE: Instead of using
the vinegar and olive oil for the dressing, mix 2 teaspoons Dijon mustard
into ½ cup mayonnaise and stir until well blended. Spoon about 1½
tablespoons of dressing on each serving. ⌒

CRAB OR SHRIMP LOUIE

....

—✑ Always a favorite salad of mine, and one that is reminiscent of days gone by and trips made to Fisherman's Wharf in San Francisco. For more nostalgia, serve with sourdough French bread.

2 tablespoons olive oil
2 tablespoons rice vinegar
1/8 teaspoon cayenne
1 teaspoon prepared mustard
2 hard-boiled eggs, chopped fine
1 teaspoon minced fresh parsley
1 cup finely chopped celery
2 cups cooked crabmeat or shrimp *(see page 143)*, chopped in small
    pieces
Salt to taste
About 1/2 cup mayonnaise
1 head Bibb lettuce

Put the oil, vinegar, cayenne, mustard, eggs, and parsley in a mixing bowl and whisk until well blended. Add the celery and crabmeat (or shrimp), and toss together until all the ingredients are coated with the dressing. Season with salt to taste and add enough mayonnaise to coat and moisten all the ingredients; toss again to mix well. Chill and serve on leaves of Bibb lettuce. ✑

POPPY SEED DRESSING

⟿ Wonderful on spinach salad, shredded carrots, or a simple green salad tossed with blue cheese.

1½ cups sugar
2 teaspoons dry mustard
2 teaspoons salt
⅔ cup cider vinegar
3 tablespoons onion juice
2 cups vegetable oil
3 tablespoons poppy seed

Mix all of the ingredients thoroughly in a jar with a tight lid by shaking well. Store in the refrigerator. ⟿

VERY GOOD SALAD DRESSING

This dressing also doubles as a very good barbecue sauce. My husband used to grill chicken using this sauce, and called it "Blackened Chicken," because he liked it charred with lots of sauce. Along with the chicken, he would eat a wedge of iceberg lettuce drenched with the dressing. By the way, he said this was the only green thing he liked besides money. In any case, be sure to be generous whether you decide to use this as a dressing or a sauce.

One 10¾-ounce can condensed tomato soup
¾ cup cider vinegar
1 teaspoon dry mustard
1 tablespoon Worcestershire sauce
2 tablespoons grated onion
2 cloves garlic, peeled
1 cup olive oil
¾ cup vegetable oil
¾ cup sugar

Put all of the ingredients in a blender and blend thoroughly. Store in the refrigerator until ready to use.

GREEN GODDESS DRESSING

᠆ᕐᕐ Around 1925, George Arliss starred in the play *The Green Goddess*. The chef at the Palace Hotel in San Francisco honored Arliss by creating a creamy dressing for a green salad called "Green Goddess." It gained great popularity, which it still richly deserves.

One 2-ounce tin anchovies
3 tablespoons chopped fresh chives
3 tablespoons tarragon vinegar
1 tablespoon lemon juice
1 cup sour cream
1 cup mayonnaise
1/2 cup chopped fresh parsley
1/2 teaspoon salt
Black pepper to taste

Put all of the ingredients in a blender and blend until smooth. Cover and refrigerate until needed. Refrigerate for up to 1 week. ᕐᕔ

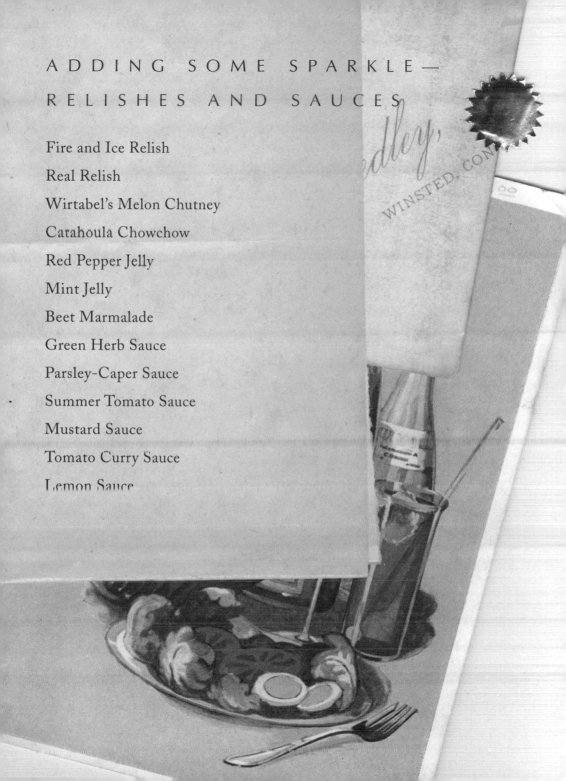

ADDING SOME SPARKLE—
RELISHES AND SAUCES

Fire and Ice Relish

Real Relish

Wirtabel's Melon Chutney

Catahoula Chowchow

Red Pepper Jelly

Mint Jelly

Beet Marmalade

Green Herb Sauce

Parsley-Caper Sauce

Summer Tomato Sauce

Mustard Sauce

Tomato Curry Sauce

Lemon Sauce

Not many of us are putting up relishes anymore, but they add such sparkle to a simple meal that I urge you to try making some. It's a good way to liven up dull leftovers. You don't necessarily have to process these relishes if you have room to store them in your refrigerator or freezer.

It's also nice to have a few sauces, such as the ones you'll find in this chapter, to dress up cold meats or yesterday's vegetables, or to toss with pasta.

FIRE AND ICE RELISH

⟶ഌ This relish was all the rage during the 1940s. Little dishes of Fire and Ice Relish kept dainty lunches company in tearooms all over California. Today, I like to serve it with cold chicken, meat loaf, or salmon. It's amazing what a great addition it is to sandwiches as well.

3 cups cherry tomatoes (about 3/4 pound)
1 large green bell pepper
1 large red onion
1/4 cup cider vinegar
4 teaspoons sugar
1 1/2 teaspoons celery seed
1 1/2 teaspoons mustard seed
1/2 teaspoon salt
1/2 teaspoon black pepper
1/8 teaspoon cayenne
1/4 cup water

Cut the cherry tomatoes in half, or, if they are large, into quarters, and put in a bowl. Seed, remove the ribs, and coarsely chop the green pepper and toss in with the tomatoes. Finely chop the onion and add it to the bowl.

Mix together the cider vinegar, sugar, celery seed, mustard seed, salt, pepper, and cayenne with the water in a small saucepan and bring to a boil. Boil for 1 minute. Remove from the heat and immediately pour over the prepared vegetables. Let cool, then cover and refrigerate for at least 3 hours before serving.

This is a fresh relish and will keep no more than a day or two. However, you can freeze the leftover relish in small Baggies and take them out of the freezer as needed. ഌ⟵

REAL RELISH

—◦ A relish that has withstood the test of time, from a recipe that's been around since at least the 1920s. It's a benchmark for basic relish. It's sweet and spicy, and the best relish for beef.

1 pound tomatoes, chopped
1 medium onion, chopped
2 ribs celery, chopped
1 green bell pepper, seeded, ribs removed, and chopped
Salt
1 cup cider vinegar
1 cup sugar
2 teaspoons mustard seed
1 tablespoon pickling spice

Put the tomatoes, onion, celery, and green pepper in a large bowl, lightly salt, and toss until blended.

Put the vinegar, sugar, mustard seed, pickling spice, and 1 teaspoon salt in a saucepan and bring to a boil. Reduce the heat and let this pickling brine simmer for 2 to 3 minutes. Remove from the heat and strain the hot brine over the vegetable mixture. Stir, then put the relish into clean jars. Cover and refrigerate until needed. If keeping for longer than 2 weeks, it can be frozen. ◦—

WIRTABEL'S MELON CHUTNEY

⌐ My friend Wirtabel's family makes this chutney every year with the unripened melons on their farm. It is excellent, and beats mango chutney by a mile—it's far less expensive to make, too.

12 cups peeled, seeded, and diced fruit*
1 cup golden raisins and 1 cup dark raisins, mixed
1 cup peeled, chopped fresh ginger
4½ cups sugar
3 cups white vinegar
1 teaspoon whole allspice
½ teaspoon whole cloves
2 cinnamon sticks, each about 2 inches long

*Use about 6 cups ripe or unripe cantaloupe or honeydew melon cut into
1-inch cubes; the remaining fruit may be pears, apples, or peaches.

Mix together the fruit, raisins, ginger, sugar, and vinegar in a large Dutch oven or heavy saucepan. Tie the allspice, cloves, and cinnamon sticks in a piece of cheesecloth. Use a hammer to smash the spices in the cheesecloth a couple of times to release more flavor during cooking. Tuck the bag of spices into the fruit in the Dutch oven.

Bring the mixture to a boil, stirring occasionally. Reduce the heat to a simmer and cook for about 2 hours, until the chutney has thickened and turned darker. Taste occasionally to check on the need for more spices or sugar or salt. When thick and dark, remove from the heat and discard the spice bag.

Put the hot chutney into clean hot jars, cover, and refrigerate when cool. The chutney will keep for up to 1 month. For longer preserving, fill hot, sterilized jars with the hot mixture, leaving a ¼-inch headspace. Put on the lids and tighten, and process in a boiling-water bath for 15 minutes. ⌐

CATAHOULA CHOWCHOW

—᠗ Chowchow is such a treat to serve with hot or cold meats. This recipe makes a large amount, and if you don't have much storage, you can cut the proportions in half. But if you're going to the trouble of "putting up" this delicious relish, why not give some jars to friends?

2$^{1}/_{2}$ pounds green tomatoes, chopped
2$^{1}/_{2}$ pounds pickling cucumbers, chopped
4 cups chopped yellow onions
2 cups chopped celery ribs
3 green bell peppers, seeded, ribs removed, and chopped
1 small green cabbage, thinly sliced
$^{3}/_{4}$ cup pickling, pure granulated, or kosher salt
8 cups boiling water
8 cups white vinegar
$^{1}/_{4}$ cup mustard seed
$^{1}/_{4}$ cup ground turmeric
1 tablespoon ground allspice
1 tablespoon black pepper
1 tablespoon ground cloves

Mix together the tomatoes, cucumbers, onions, celery, green peppers, and cabbage in a large bowl. Pour boiling salted water over the vegetables and let stand for 1 hour, then drain and rinse well with cold water.

Place the remaining ingredients in a large kettle or stockpot and bring to a boil. Add the vegetables and cook, stirring occasionally, until almost tender, about 20 minutes. Pack the vegetables and liquid into hot, sterilized pint jars, leaving a $^{1}/_{2}$-inch headspace, and seal according to manufacturer's directions. Process for 5 minutes in a boiling-water bath.

᠗

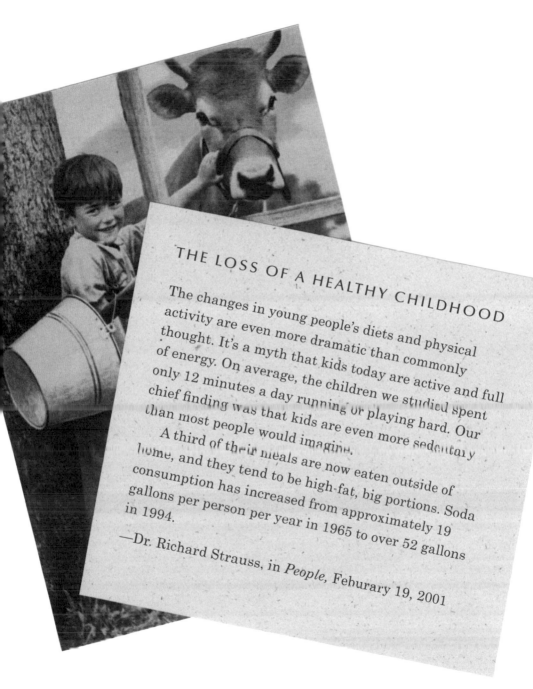

THE LOSS OF A HEALTHY CHILDHOOD

The changes in young people's diets and physical activity are even more dramatic than commonly thought. It's a myth that kids today are active and full of energy. On average, the children we studied spent only 12 minutes a day running or playing hard. Our chief finding was that kids are even more sedentary than most people would imagine.

A third of their meals are now eaten outside of home, and they tend to be high-fat, big portions. Soda consumption has increased from approximately 19 gallons per person per year in 1965 to over 52 gallons in 1994.

—Dr. Richard Strauss, in *People*, Feburary 19, 2001

RED PEPPER JELLY

⤙ Red bell pepper, chili powder, and a pinch of cayenne give this jelly its heat, while the sugar adds a balanced sweetness. Try this jelly on corn bread—you'll be surprised at what a good accompaniment it is!

2½ pounds red bell peppers
1 tablespoon salt
3 to 4 tablespoons chili powder
1 cup fresh lemon juice
2 cups cider vinegar
2 packages powdered pectin
¼ to ½ teaspoon cayenne
10 cups sugar (5-pound bag)

Cut the red peppers in quarters and remove the seeds. Grind them in a food processor until very finely chopped. Transfer them to a saucepan and add all of the rest of the ingredients except the sugar. Bring to a boil and cook, stirring occasionally, for 10 minutes.

Add the sugar and stir, bring to a boil again, and let the mixture boil just long enough to dissolve the sugar. Pour into hot, sterilized jelly jars and seal. ⌀

MINT JELLY

MAKES 4 CUPS

Still perfect with a rack or roast leg of lamb, Mint Jelly can be made and kept for months. Fresh mint is crucial to the flavor of this jelly. It can be spread on biscuits or served with fish, chicken, ham, or root vegetables.

1 cup chopped fresh mint
1 cup boiling water
3½ cups sugar
¾ cup water
¼ cup cider vinegar
4 drops of green food coloring
1 pouch (3 ounces) Certo

Make an infusion of the mint and the boiling water by simmering them together uncovered for 10 minutes. Strain through a cloth-lined strainer.

Combine 1½ cups of the mint infusion with the sugar, water, vinegar, and food coloring in a saucepan and bring to a boil.

Add the Certo and bring to a boil again, stirring constantly. Boil for about 1 minute, and pour into hot, sterilized canning jars. Set lids on top and seal.

BEET MARMALADE

....

MAKES 4 CUPS

⤳ Every time I make this, I am amazed at how fast it disappears. It is particularly good with roast chicken or turkey.

4 medium-large beets
1¹/₂ cups sugar
1 large lemon
2 tablespoons chopped peeled fresh ginger

Cut the leaves off the beets, leaving 1 inch of stems on the root ends. Wash the beets thoroughly. Bring a large pot of salted water to a boil, add the beets, and cover. Cook until the beets are easily pierced with a knife—this can be anywhere from 35 to 60 minutes, depending on the age of the beets. Drain the beets, rinse them with cool water, and allow them to cool slightly before peeling off the skins with your hands or a small paring knife. Cut into large chunks, then put the beets in a food processor and process until coarsely chopped, or mash by hand.

Transfer the beets to a heavy-bottomed saucepan and stir in the sugar. Put the lemon and ginger in the food processor and process until finely chopped, or chop finely by hand. Add the lemon and ginger to the beet mixture and stir to blend. Set the pan over medium-low heat, cover, and cook, stirring often, until the marmalade has thickened a little. This will take about 2 minutes, and the marmalade will get thicker as it cools.

For keeping no longer than 1 month, put the hot marmalade into clean jars, cover, and refrigerate. For longer preserving, pour or spoon into hot, sterilized jars, leaving a ¹/₄-inch headspace, and seal. Process in a boiling-water bath for 15 minutes. ⌒

GREEN HERB SAUCE

—⟳ Also known as coriander or Chinese parsley, cilantro appeared in China around 200 B.C. and is the premier herb in China, India, Africa, and Latin America. Now it has also become a Western staple. Green Herb Sauce is a perfect way to enhance simple foods. Spoon it over a piece of grilled chicken or fish, or stir it into a soup that needs added flavor. It is best served the day it's made. You could make just half the amount in a mini food processor if that's all you'll be needing.

5 cloves garlic, peeled
3 tablespoons grated lemon peel
1 cup fresh cilantro leaves
1 cup chopped fresh parsley
1 cup olive oil
1 teaspoon salt
1/2 teaspoon black pepper

Put all of the ingredients in a food processor and process until smooth. ⟳

PARSLEY-CAPER SAUCE

 Sharp and lemony, this sauce brightens warm or cold vegetables, fried cheese, vegetable fritters, and grains and beans.

1/2 cup finely chopped fresh parsley
2 tablespoons small capers, rinsed
1 shallot, finely diced
1 teaspoon grated lemon peel
1/3 cup extra-virgin olive oil
1 tablespoon white wine vinegar or champagne vinegar
2 teaspoons lemon juice (or to taste)
Salt and black pepper to taste

Whisk everything together, using enough salt and pepper to suit your taste. Let stand for 10 minutes, then taste again and adjust the seasonings, adding more vinegar or lemon juice if needed. Serve right away.

An Aphorism of the Professor

He who plays host without giving his personal care to
the repast is unworthy of having friends to invite to it.

—Jean Anthelme Brillat-Savarin,
from the preamble to *The Physiology of Taste*

SUMMER TOMATO SAUCE

⚯ This pasta sauce requires no cooking, and it is most flavorful in the summer when the ripest tomatoes and basil are available. Serve it over hot pasta, or allow the pasta to cool before tossing it with the sauce to make a wonderful cold pasta dish for your next picnic.

2 large cloves garlic
1/2 teaspoon coarse salt or plain salt
2 green onions (scallions)
2 large tomatoes or 5 small Roma or plum tomatoes
4 fresh parsley sprigs
6 fresh basil leaves
3 tablespoons olive oil

Peel the cloves of garlic and put them on a chopping board. Cut each clove into 4 pieces. Sprinkle the garlic with salt and chop into tiny pieces. (The salt will catch the garlic juice and help flavor your sauce.) Put the chopped garlic in a large mixing bowl.

Cut all but 2 inches of the green onion tops off and remove the bottom roots. Chop the onions into small pieces and add to the chopped garlic. Core the tomatoes, cut them in half, then dice. Add them to the mixing bowl.

Chop the parsley and basil finely and add them to the mixing bowl. Stir in the olive oil and mix well.

Taste your fresh sauce and add more salt if it seems to taste "blah," and mix it well. ⚯

MUSTARD SAUCE

⤙ Mustard Sauce can add flavor to a number of dishes. Mix it with warm potatoes and fresh dill for a potato salad, pour it over roasted chicken or fish, or drizzle a little over fresh greens for a simple salad. This is a breeze to make, but you need to taste and correct the sauce so it seems balanced and tasty. There should be just a hint of sweetness.

1½ tablespoons minced fresh parsley
Juice of 1 lemon
1 tablespoon Dijon mustard
1 cup heavy cream
Pinch of cayenne
Sugar to taste
Salt to taste

Whisk the parsley, lemon juice, mustard, cream, and cayenne, to blend well. Taste and add a pinch of sugar and a pinch of salt. Add more sugar and salt if necessary. If you are serving this with a hot dish like fish or timbales, warm the sauce until it is hot, but don't let it boil. ⤚

TOMATO CURRY SAUCE

—☙ Although this sauce is normally served over chicken, it can be one of your favorite sauces used on its own. Serve it over pasta or rice for a tasty side dish, or add pieces of cooked chicken or pork to make it an entrée.

4 tablespoons (1/2 stick) butter
1/3 cup finely diced onion
1/3 cup finely diced green bell pepper
1 clove garlic, crushed
1 tablespoon curry powder
1/2 teaspoon crumbled dried thyme
One 16-ounce can stewed tomatoes, chopped, with their liquid
1 teaspoon salt
1/4 teaspoon black pepper

Melt the butter in a skillet, and add the onion, green pepper, garlic, curry powder, and thyme. Cook, stirring, over medium heat until the vegetables are softened. Add the stewed tomatoes and their liquid and gently simmer for 5 minutes. You may need to add some water if the sauce becomes too thick. Season with salt and pepper to taste. ☙

LEMON SAUCE

⎯◌ Pale yellow, with a nice lemon bite. This sauce is good over cauliflower, spinach, or broccoli. Just a touch brightens the taste of many different dishes.

¹/₂ cup chicken broth
1¹/₂ teaspoons butter
1 tablespoon cornstarch
2 tablespoons cold water
1 egg yolk, lightly beaten
1¹/₂ tablespoons lemon juice
Grated rind of ¹/₂ lemon

Heat the chicken broth and butter in a heavy-bottomed pan. In a small dish, blend the cornstarch with the cold water until smooth; slowly stir this mixture into the chicken broth. Cook, stirring constantly, over low heat for 5 minutes, or until the broth is thickened and smooth. Beat 2 tablespoons of the thickened broth into the egg yolk, then stir the broth-yolk mixture back into the broth. Add the lemon juice and rind, and cook gently for 1 minute more. Do not boil. This sauce will keep for a couple of days if it is well covered in the refrigerator. It can be reheated by stirring over low heat. ◌⎯

PUDDINGS, CAKES, COOKIES, AND CANDIES— THE TASTE MEMORIES OF CHILDHOOD

Truman's Ozark Pudding

Frozen Maple Mousse

Summer Pudding

Bread and Butter Pudding

Creamy Rice with
   Maple Syrup

Rhubarb Betty

American Apple Pie

Shoofly Pie

Crêpes Suzette

Strawberry Shortcake

Lemon Pudding Cake

Chocolate Social Cake

Brownstone Front Cake

Lazy Daisy Cake

Hoosier Cake

Pineapple Upside-Down Cake

Blue Ribbon Gingerbread

Baked Alaska

Children's Chocolate-Chip
   Squares

Caramel-Covered Stuffed
   Date Rolls

Hermits

Schrafft's Butterscotch Cookies

Chocolate Icebox Cookies

Dainty Pralines

Candied Grapefruit Peel

Desserts, above all, are apt to evoke memories of childhood, of sitting around a family table and waiting for the crowning moment when a cake or a pudding or a pie would be brought out. Ask anyone what their favorite recipe is and it is bound to be a sweet. I know that my favorite is the Lazy Daisy Cake that my mother used to make. She wasn't the cook that my grandmother was, but it's hard to miss with that cake, and she took great pride in it. James Beard was partial to Brownstone cakes (he had several of them in his books), and my editor, Judith Jones, remembers fondly summers in Vermont when they would eat a succession of summer puddings made with white bread and berries that changed as the season progressed.

So try some of these old favorites and give your children taste memories they will cherish forever.

TRUMAN'S OZARK PUDDING

....

SERVES 6

—⌒ President Harry Truman loved Ozark Pudding, which his wife, Bess, often made for him. It was called "Bess Truman's Ozark Pudding" and was especially popular with all the Democrats.

1 egg
3/4 cup sugar
2 tablespoons all-purpose flour
1¼ teaspoons baking powder
¼ teaspoon salt
½ cup chopped peeled apples
½ cup chopped nuts
1 teaspoon vanilla
Whipped cream (with a touch of rum, if desired) or
    vanilla ice cream

Preheat the oven to 350 degrees. Grease a 10-inch pie pan.

Beat the egg and the sugar together until smooth. Add the flour, baking powder, and salt. Blend well. Fold in the apples, nuts, and vanilla. Pour into the prepared pie pan and bake for 30 to 35 minutes. Remove from the oven; the pudding will fall, but it's supposed to. Serve warm with whipped cream or ice cream. ⌒—

FROZEN MAPLE MOUSSE

SERVES 6

⟶ Although this rich and pure maple-tasting mousse should be put in the freezer for four hours or more, it will have a more pleasing texture if you remove it from the freezer an hour before serving and refrigerate.

1 cup maple syrup
2 egg whites, at room temperature
Pinch of salt
1 cup heavy cream

Put the maple syrup in a 1-quart saucepan over medium heat. Meanwhile, beat the egg whites in a very clean bowl with the salt until they hold firm peaks. Watch the syrup carefully now; as the large bubbles start to turn into smaller bubbles and when you lift a spoon with syrup in it 8 inches or so above the pan and the falling syrup spins a thread, remove immediately from the heat (it should be about 260 degrees if you're using a candy thermometer). With the electric beater going, pour the hot syrup in a thin, steady stream into the egg whites. In a separate bowl, beat the cream, preferably over a bowl of ice to get greater volume, until it forms soft peaks, and then fold it into the maple–egg white mixture. Turn into a pretty bowl or sherbet glasses and freeze for 2 hours or more before serving. ⟳

SUMMER PUDDING

⎯☙ Summer puddings are made with berries: raspberries, blackberries, or blueberries. This is a glorious dessert, and you really don't even have to know how to cook to make it.

7 thin slices white bread, plus more if needed
Softened butter
5 cups blueberries (or any combination of blackberries,
    raspberries, and blueberries)
1/2 to 2/3 cup sugar
1/3 cup water

Butter one side of 6 slices of the bread very lightly. Place the slices, butter side out, around the sides of a round 3- to 4-cup bowl. Fill the gaps with bread trimmed to fit so the bowl is completely covered.

Cook the blueberries with the sugar (adjust the amount according to the sweetness of the berries) and the water for 10 minutes, then pour them into the bread-lined bowl. Place the unbuttered slice of bread on top and fold the edges of the other slices over to cover the fruit completely. Place a saucer on top and press down. Pour off the excess liquid and reserve it to serve with the pudding. Chill the pudding for at least 6 hours before serving. ☙⎯

BREAD AND BUTTER PUDDING

—⌒ Bread and Butter Pudding is a very old English dessert that has many variations, but this recipe is my all-time favorite. It used to be served at the legendary New York restaurant The Coach House—James Beard could never resist ordering it.

6 slices French bread (not sourdough), crusts removed
4 tablespoons (1/2 stick) butter, room temperature
3 eggs
2 egg yolks
1/2 cup sugar
1/4 teaspoon salt
2 cups milk
1/2 cup heavy cream
1 1/2 teaspoons vanilla
Confectioners' sugar for sprinkling

Preheat the oven to 375 degrees. Have ready a 2-quart baking dish. Butter one side of each slice of bread and set aside.

Put the eggs, yolks, sugar, and salt in a large bowl and beat until thoroughly mixed. Pour the milk and cream into a heavy-bottomed saucepan and heat until scalded (tiny bubbles will form around the edges of the pan). Remove from the heat and, whisking briskly, slowly add the egg mixture. Stir in the vanilla.

Put a kettle of water on to boil.

Layer the bread, butter side up, in the baking dish. Strain the custard into the dish (the bread will float to the top). Set the baking dish in a larger pan and place on the middle rack of the oven. Pull out the rack just enough so that you can pour boiling water into the pan—the water should come halfway up the sides of the baking dish.

Bake for about 45 minutes, or until the custard is set except for a slight tremble in the center. Remove from the oven and sprinkle confectioners' sugar on top. It is delicious hot or cold, and just perfect with a little unsweetened heavy cream poured over it. ⌒

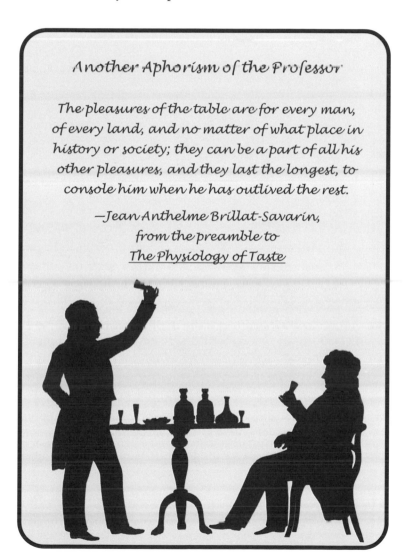

Another Aphorism of the Professor

The pleasures of the table are for every man, of every land, and no matter of what place in history or society; they can be a part of all his other pleasures, and they last the longest, to console him when he has outlived the rest.

—Jean Anthelme Brillat-Savarin, from the preamble to *The Physiology of Taste*

CREAMY RICE WITH
MAPLE SYRUP

···

⌐⌐ Snowy white rice, sweet and creamy, plus it is a breeze to make.

1/2 cup long-grain rice
1 1/2 cups milk
3 or 4 cardamom seeds *(optional)*
1 cup heavy cream
1/4 cup sugar, preferably superfine
1/2 teaspoon vanilla
About 3/4 cup maple syrup

Put the rice in a small, heavy saucepan, pour 1 cup of the milk over, and drop in the cardamom seeds, if using. Bring to a boil, then reduce the heat, cover, and simmer gently for about 15 minutes, or until the milk is absorbed. Stir gently with a fork, add the remaining 1/2 cup milk, and simmer again, covered, for 15 to 20 minutes, until the milk is absorbed; if it isn't, simmer uncovered, stirring occasionally, until it has all evaporated. Fluff the rice up with a fork and let cool completely, first at room temperature, then in the refrigerator.

Whip the cream, preferably over a bowl of ice cubes, until it thickens, then add the sugar and continue to beat until the cream forms firm peaks. Stir in the vanilla and fold the whipped cream into the cooled rice. Pack the mixture into 4 individual molds and chill thoroughly.

To serve, unmold onto plates and pass the maple syrup in a pitcher to pour on top. ⌐⌐

RHUBARB BETTY

—୵ Everyone has probably heard of Apple Brown Betty, but Rhubarb Betty is a nice change for those who love rhubarb. Bettys date back to colonial America, and they are really just baked puddings made of layers of sugar and fruit, and buttered bread crumbs. Rhubarb Betty is a nice contrast of sweet and tart. It is particularly delicious served with sliced strawberries and cream.

4 slices bread, crusts removed
2 pounds rhubarb stalks, trimmed (don't peel) and
    cut into 2-inch pieces
1^1/$_2$ cups sugar
^{1}/$_4$ cup water
6 tablespoons (^{3}/$_4$ stick) butter, melted
2 cups sliced fresh strawberries *(optional)*
Pitcher of heavy cream *(optional)*

Preheat the oven to 350 degrees.

Lay the bread slices in a single layer in the preheated oven. Check every 5 minutes, turning the slices once, and toast until golden on both sides. Remove and let cool. Make into coarse crumbs by blending briefly in the food processor or grating through the largest holes of a grater.

Place the rhubarb in a saucepan with the sugar and the water, cover, and cook until tender, about 5 minutes. Set aside.

Put the bread crumbs in a bowl with the melted butter and toss to coat all the crumbs. Spread the cooked rhubarb in an 8-inch square baking dish. Sprinkle the crumbs evenly over the top and bake for about 30 minutes, or until the crumbs are browned.

To serve, if you are using the sliced strawberries, put a large spoonful of them on a dessert plate, then place a portion of the warm Rhubarb Betty alongside them. Pass the pitcher of cream. ୵

AMERICAN APPLE PIE

....

—◌ Serve this pie warm with a slice of Cheddar cheese or ice cream or whipped cream.

DOUGH

2$\frac{1}{2}$ cups all-purpose flour
$\frac{1}{2}$ teaspoon salt
$\frac{3}{4}$ cup vegetable shortening (I use Crisco)
6 to 7 tablespoons cold water

APPLE FILLING

$\frac{3}{4}$ cup sugar
1 teaspoon ground cinnamon
$\frac{1}{4}$ teaspoon ground allspice
$\frac{1}{4}$ teaspoon ground nutmeg
1 tablespoon all-purpose flour
1$\frac{1}{2}$ pounds apples, peeled, cored, and sliced about
    $\frac{1}{8}$ inch thick (about 6 cups) *(see Note)*
1 tablespoon lemon juice
3 tablespoons butter, cut into small pieces

To make the pastry dough, put the flour and salt in a mixing bowl; using a fork to stir, distribute the salt throughout the flour. Add the shortening and break into small chunks. Either lightly rub the chunks into small pieces throughout the flour or use a pastry blender to cut the shortening into the flour. Mix lightly until the mixture resembles coarse meal. The texture won't be uniform but will be made up of small pieces and crumbs. Sprinkle the water over the flour mixture 1 tablespoon at a time, mixing lightly with the fork; add only enough water so the dough will hold together when pressed gently into a ball. If there are dry places that don't adhere, sprinkle a little more water over them. Put the dough in a bowl, cover, and chill in the refrigerator while you prepare the apples.

To make the apple filling, put the sugar, cinnamon, allspice, nutmeg, and flour in a large mixing bowl. Add the apples and the lemon juice, and toss together gently but thoroughly.

Preheat the oven to 425 degrees.

Divide the dough in half. Roll out one half about 2 inches larger than the pie pan. Transfer the dough to the pan, fitting it in loosely but firmly all around.

Fill the pie shell with the apple mixture, mounding it somewhat higher in the center. Although the apple filling may appear quite high, it will shrink considerably during the baking. Dot the top of the filling with the butter.

Roll out the remaining half of the dough into a circle the same size and thickness as the bottom crust. Roll it up on the rolling pin, and then unroll, starting at the edge of the pie and letting it drop so it is draped over the filling. With scissors, trim the top crust, leaving about 1/4 inch of crust over the edge of the pie pan. Tuck the overhanging 1/4 inch under the edge of the bottom crust all around the rim and then press down with the tines of a fork to seal the two crusts together. Cut two small gashes in the center of the top crust to allow the steam to escape.

Place the pie on the middle rack of the preheated oven and bake for 30 minutes. Reduce the heat to 350 degrees and continue baking for 20 to 30 minutes more. The pie is done when the apples are soft. Test by piercing through the gashes into the apples to make sure they are tender. If the pie starts to become too dark, cover loosely with aluminum foil.

NOTE: It's important to use fresh-tasting, crisp apples. I find Fuji apples particularly dependable, and Royal Gala can be good, too. ✑

SHOOFLY PIE

—⟨ A splendid pie for the thrifty, with a moist caramel-like filling and a crispy crumb topping, it can be ready to bake with barely a "flick of the whisk." Shoofly Pie is Pennsylvania Dutch in origin, and no one seems to be certain just how it got its name.

Basic Pastry Dough *(page 95)*
1 cup all-purpose flour
1/2 cup packed light brown sugar
1/2 cup vegetable shortening
1 cup water
1 teaspoon baking soda
1 cup dark corn syrup
1/2 teaspoon salt
1/2 cup heavy cream, softly whipped

Preheat the oven to 350 degrees. Line a 9-inch pie pan with the rolled-out dough.

To make the crumb topping, put the flour, brown sugar, and shortening in a bowl. Using a pastry blender, two knives, or your fingertips, work the shortening into the flour and sugar until the mixture resembles small crumbs.

Pour the water into a small saucepan and bring to a boil. Remove the pan from the heat and stir in the baking soda. Add the corn syrup and salt, and blend well. Pour this filling into the pie shell and sprinkle the crumb topping evenly over the top. Bake for about 40 minutes, or until the filling is set. Serve warm with the whipped cream. ⟨⟩

HOW WE LIVE TODAY

Today's mania for take-out food and the disappearance of home cooking have two related causes—smaller households and working women. (No man ever gave up cooking because he went back to work.) Are these trends likely to continue? With the aid of a see-through plastic ruler, I have projected the past twenty-five years of U.S. Census Bureau figures into the future, and the results are chilling.

Item: By the year 2050 the average family size will have decreased to about one person. Everyone in America will be living alone.

Item: All women older than eighteen will be working outside the home.

Item: All women will be older than eighteen.

The inevitable conclusion is that by the year 2050, everybody will order take-out food at every meal.

Eating will become extremely expensive. You will need an annual income of at least $392,114 in current dollars to get by. Grazing my way from one end of Manhattan to the other, I found that a modestly upscale take-out breakfast, lunch, and dinner cost $40 plus $7 for a taxi or $54,896 a year for an average family of 3.2 persons. Department of Agriculture figures show that the average American family spends 14 percent of its income on food. Therefore, it must earn $392,114 a year.

Finding good take-out food is not easy. Searching it out will become your full-time occupation in the year 2050, more than cooking ever was. Americans will once again become a lonely race of Mesolithic hunter-gatherers prowling the darkened city streets, wallets honed and sharpened, ready to pounce on the unsuspecting pint of pasta primavera and snare the slow-footed slice of *pâté de campagne*. We will scarcely have time to eat.

—Jeffrey Steingarten, *The Man Who Ate Everything*

CRÊPES SUZETTE

⸺ This classic French dessert—homemade crêpes drenched in a citrus-butter sauce—is not made much anymore. In the past, it was often the finale to an elegant meal, finished with a flourish, usually by the man of the house as he poured the brandy into the chafing dish and set it aflame at the table. It may seem demanding to produce, but if you make the crêpe batter the night before, as I do, giving the flour a chance to relax and absorb the liquid, and then cook the crêpes a few hours before serving, it is really pretty simple to put together. If you have extra crêpes, they are very good filled with creamed chicken or seafood, or with fresh berries and topped with whipped cream.

CRÊPE BATTER

2 cups milk
4 tablespoons (1/2 stick) unsalted butter
1/2 teaspoon sugar
1/4 teaspoon salt
1 1/4 cups all-purpose flour
1 tablespoon vegetable oil
3 eggs
1/2 cup beer

SYRUP

2 teaspoons grated orange peel
1 teaspoon grated lemon peel
1/2 cup orange juice
8 tablespoons sugar
4 tablespoons (1/2 stick) butter
1/4 cup Grand Marnier or other orange-flavored liqueur, warmed
1/4 cup Cognac, warmed

LOST RECIPES / 188

To make the crêpes, heat the milk, butter, sugar, and salt in a saucepan until the butter has melted. Put the flour in a mixing bowl, make a well in it, pour in the vegetable oil, then break in the eggs. Mix lightly with a whisk or an electric beater until the mixture starts to thicken. Add the warm milk mixture little by little, beating until smooth. Mix in the beer and strain the batter into a refrigerator container. Refrigerate for at least 2 hours, or overnight (it will keep for up to 5 days).

To fry the crêpes, let the batter come to room temperature. Rub a crêpe pan or a skillet lightly with butter and wipe it out with a paper towel. Heat the pan until a drop of water thrown into it sizzles. Ladle about 2 tablespoons of the batter into the center of the pan, then lift, tilt, and rotate the pan immediately so the batter runs to the edges and covers the bottom evenly. Cook the crêpe over medium-high heat until lightly browned on the bottom—it will take about 1 minute—then turn it by lifting the edge and easing it over with a spatula. Cook the second side for about 1 minute and turn it out onto a piece of plastic wrap. Repeat until you have used up all of the batter.

Using 12 of the crêpes (if you have extra, save them for another day), fold them in half, paler side down, and lay them overlapping on a plate.

To make the syrup, mix the orange and lemon peel with the juice in a small bowl. (Bring this to the table if you are planning to do the finish there.)

Melt 6 tablespoons of the sugar in a 10- or 12-inch skillet or chafing dish over high heat, shaking the pan frequently, until the sugar turns amber, about 2 minutes. Reduce the heat to low and add the peel and juice all at once; the sugar will harden, so stir until it dissolves. Add the butter and stir until melted. Now tuck the folded crêpes into the pan and baste them with the syrup, sprinkle with the remaining 2 tablespoons sugar, pour on the Grand Marnier and Cognac, and, if you like the drama of setting them ablaze at the table, carefully strike a match to burn off the alcohol. When the flames die down, serve immediately. ⌒

STRAWBERRY SHORTCAKE

3 pints strawberries
1 cup sugar
6 Cream Biscuits *(page 37)*
1¹/₂ cups heavy cream, whipped

Rinse the berries with cold water. Hull and slice them into a bowl. Sprinkle ¹/₂ cup of the sugar over the berries and toss to distribute the sugar over all. Let stand for 5 minutes, toss again, and taste. Add more sugar if the strawberries still don't seem sweet enough.

Split the biscuits in half, then put 2 halves, split side up, on each of 6 dessert plates. Spoon the strawberries over the biscuits, top with whipped cream, and serve. ⌒

LEMON PUDDING CAKE

—⟶ This lovely, light dessert is an old favorite of mine from days past. The batter is mixed together in one bowl and the magic transformation happens in the oven—a creamy lemon pudding forms on the bottom and a light sponge cake emerges on top.

1 cup sugar
1/8 teaspoon salt
1/4 cup all-purpose flour
4 tablespoons (1/2 stick) butter, melted
1/3 cup freshly squeezed lemon juice
Grated peel of 1 lemon
3 eggs, separated
1 1/2 cups milk
Heavy cream *(optional)*

Preheat the oven to 350 degrees. Butter a 1 1/2-quart baking dish or an 8-inch square baking pan.

Mix 3/4 cup of the sugar, the salt, and the flour together in a bowl. Add the melted butter, lemon juice, lemon peel, and egg yolks, and stir until thoroughly blended. Stir in the milk. In a separate bowl, beat the egg whites with the remaining 1/4 cup sugar until they are stiff but remain moist. Fold the beaten whites into the lemon mixture, then pour the batter into the prepared baking dish.

Set the baking dish in a larger pan at least 2 inches deep and pour enough hot water into the larger pan to come halfway up the sides of the baking dish. Bake for about 45 minutes, or until the top is lightly browned.

Serve warm or chilled, with heavy cream, if you wish. ⟶

CHOCOLATE SOCIAL CAKE

This is everything a classic chocolate cake should be. Rich with butter, deeply flavored with chocolate, and finished with fluffy whipped cream.

CAKE

7 ounces (7 squares) unsweetened chocolate
12 tablespoons (1½ sticks) butter
1½ cups cold strong coffee
¼ cup water
2 eggs
1 teaspoon vanilla
2 cups flour (cake flour if possible)
1½ cups sugar
1 teaspoon baking soda
¼ teaspoon salt

TOPPING

2 cups heavy cream
2 teaspoons vanilla

Preheat the oven to 275 degrees. Grease and lightly flour two 8½ by 4½-inch loaf pans.

Put the chocolate, butter, and coffee in a large, heavy-bottomed saucepan. Place over low heat and stir constantly until the chocolate melts, then stir vigorously to blend and smooth the mixture completely. Set aside to cool for about 10 minutes, then beat in the water, eggs, and vanilla. Sift the flour, sugar, baking soda, and salt together. Add the dry ingredients to the chocolate mixture, and beat with a wooden spoon or a wire whisk until the batter is well blended and smooth.

Divide the batter evenly between the two prepared pans, and bake for 45 to 55 minutes, until a toothpick inserted in the center of a loaf comes out clean. Remove from the oven and let the loaves cool in the pans for about 15 minutes, then turn them out onto racks to finish cooling completely.

Before serving the cake, put the cream and vanilla in a large mixing bowl and whip until the cream just barely stands in peaks. It should be fluffy but thin enough to run down the sides of the cake when you place a spoonful on each serving. Serve each piece of cake with a generous dollop of the whipped cream. ᴔ

BROWNSTONE FRONT CAKE

....

—⌒ This is a cake of many names: Burnt Leather, Brownstone Front, and Caramel Cake, to name a few. All evolved from the fact that the caramelized sugar makes the cake a rich brown color. Regardless of what you decide to call this cake, it is intensely flavored, keeps well, and is delicious served with sliced peaches.

BURNT SUGAR SYRUP

1½ cups sugar
½ cup boiling water

CAKE

8 tablespoons (1 stick) butter, softened
1½ cups packed dark brown sugar
2 eggs, separated
2½ cups cake flour
2½ teaspoons baking powder
¼ teaspoon salt
½ cup water
Burnt Sugar Icing *(recipe follows)*

Preheat the oven to 350 degrees. Grease and lightly flour two 8-inch round cake pans.

To make the burnt sugar syrup, put the sugar in a skillet over medium heat and cook, stirring often, until the sugar has melted and turns a clear, rich brown. Slowly add the boiling water, stirring constantly. Continue to stir the syrup until it is smooth. It will be lumpy and sticky until the stirring and cooking melts and smooths the sugar. When the syrup is ready, pour it into a jar and set aside to cool.

To make the batter, put the butter in a mixing bowl and beat for a few seconds; add the brown sugar and beat until mixed (the mixture will be dry at this point). Add the egg yolks and mix well. Sift the flour, baking powder, and salt together. Add half the flour mixture to the butter-sugar mixture, then add 1/2 cup of the burnt sugar syrup mixed with the 1/2 cup water (reserve the remaining syrup for the icing). Repeat and beat until smooth. Whip the egg whites until soft peaks form. Using the electric mixer, fold the whites into the batter on the lowest speed. Fold only until barely blended.

Divide the batter evenly between the prepared pans. Bake for 20 to 25 minutes, until a knife inserted in the center of a layer comes out clean. Remove from the oven and let the layers cool in the pans for 10 minutes, then turn out onto racks to cool completely. Frost with Burnt Sugar Icing. ⌒

BURNT SUGAR ICING

MAKES 2 1/4 CUPS

8 tablespoons (1 stick) butter, softened
2 1/2 cups confectioners' sugar, sifted
1/4 teaspoon salt
6 tablespoons Burnt Sugar Syrup (the remaining syrup
    left from the Brownstone Front Cake)
About 1/2 cup heavy cream

Put the butter, confectioners' sugar, salt, and syrup in a mixing bowl. Beat until mixed—it will be very stiff at this point. Slowly add enough of the cream to make a spreadable icing. ⌒

LAZY DAISY CAKE

....

—↝ This small cake, made with hot milk, is high, light, delicate, and very easy to make. Once the hot milk has been stirred
into the batter, quickly pour it into the prepared pan and pop it
into the oven, because as soon as the baking powder is combined
with the hot liquid, it begins its work of leavening, and you want
that to happen only when it gets into the heat of the oven. (This
is not the case with cool or cold liquids.) You can omit the
broiled topping, if you wish, and frost the cake instead, once it
has cooled. But the traditional Lazy Daisy topping is very, very
good.

2 eggs
1 teaspoon vanilla
1 cup granulated sugar
1 cup all-purpose flour
1 teaspoon baking powder
1/4 teaspoon salt
1/2 cup milk
4 tablespoons (1/2 stick) butter
3 tablespoons dark brown sugar
2 tablespoons heavy cream
1/2 cup grated coconut or chopped nuts

Preheat the oven to 350 degrees. Butter and lightly flour an 8-inch square cake pan.

Beat the eggs with the vanilla until they have thickened slightly. Gradually add the granulated sugar and beat thoroughly. Mix the flour, baking powder, and salt together and add to the sugar mixture, blending until smooth. Heat the milk and 1 tablespoon of the butter together in a small saucepan. When the butter has melted, stir the milk into the batter and mix well; the batter will be very liquid. Work quickly now as noted above. Pour the batter into the prepared pan and bake for about 25 minutes, until a toothpick inserted in the center of the cake comes out clean.

Remove the cake from the oven. Mix the remaining 3 tablespoons butter, the brown sugar, the cream, and the coconut together in a small saucepan over low heat until the butter and sugar are melted and well blended. Spread over the hot cake and brown lightly under the broiler for a minute or two, taking care that the top does not burn. ∾

HOOSIER CAKE

⟶ A very sweet and fine-grained chocolate cake, with the lightest, creamiest, and fluffiest frosting imaginable—a dream of a cake recipe given to me by a fine Oregon cook, Florine Hudspeth.

1 cup granulated sugar
1 cup light brown sugar
8 tablespoons (1 stick) butter
2 eggs
1/2 cup unsweetened cocoa
1/2 cup boiling water
1 3/4 cups all-purpose flour
1 cup cold strong coffee
1 teaspoon baking soda
1 1/2 teaspoons vanilla
Gravy Icing *(recipe follows)*

Preheat the oven to 350 degrees. Grease and lightly flour two 8- or 9-inch round cake pans.

Put the granulated sugar, brown sugar, and butter in a large mixing bowl and beat until blended. Add the eggs and beat for 2 minutes, or until the mixture is smooth and creamy.

Combine the cocoa and boiling water in a small bowl and stir to blend into a creamy, thick paste. Add the cocoa mixture to the butter-sugar mixture and beat until thoroughly blended. Sprinkle on the flour and beat only until it is incorporated. Add the coffee, baking soda, and vanilla, and beat until the batter is smooth and well blended.

Divide the batter evenly between the prepared cake pans. Bake 8-inch layers for 20 to 30 minutes, 9-inch layers for about 20 minutes, or until a toothpick inserted in the center of a layer comes out clean.

Remove from the oven and let the layers cool in the pans for 5 minutes, then turn out onto racks to cool completely. Frost with Gravy Icing.

◠

GRAVY ICING

MAKES 3 CUPS

—◠ Long beating makes this frosting light and billowy. It stays soft and spreadable for days and goes well on chocolate cakes.

1 cup milk
1/3 cup all-purpose flour
1/2 pound (2 sticks) butter, softened
1 1/2 cups sugar
1 teaspoon vanilla
1 cup chopped walnuts *(optional)*

Put the milk and flour in a small, heavy-bottomed saucepan, and whisk vigorously until perfectly smooth. Bring to a boil over medium heat and boil for 1 minute, stirring constantly. The mixture will be very stiff. Remove from the heat and let stand until cool. With an electric mixer, beat the butter, sugar, and vanilla together until light and fluffy, about 5 minutes. Add the cooled milk-and-flour mixture, and continue beating until the frosting is soft, light, and fluffy, about 5 minutes more. Add the walnuts if using. You will have enough to fill and frost an 8- or 9-inch 2-layer cake. Refrigerate if you are not using it that day. ◠

PINEAPPLE UPSIDE-DOWN CAKE

⎯ↄ Pineapple Upside-Down Cake was my favorite dessert as a child. I first remember my mother making it around 1928 for special occasions. She always lacked confidence in the kitchen, especially when baking, but this cake turned out perfect every time. I loved the way it was turned upside down onto a plate so that the sticky pineapple rings with their cherries in the center were on top. It is a simple cake for a beginning baker.

1/4 cup (1/2 stick) butter
3/4 cup packed dark brown sugar
7 canned pineapple rings
7 maraschino cherries
1/3 cup vegetable shortening
2/3 cup granulated sugar
1 teaspoon vanilla
2 eggs
1 2/3 cups all-purpose flour
2 teaspoons baking powder
1/4 teaspoon salt
2/3 cup milk
Whipped cream

Preheat the oven to 350 degrees.

Melt the butter over medium heat in a 9-inch cast-iron or other ovenproof skillet. Add the brown sugar and cook, stirring constantly, until the sugar melts and is very thick and bubbly. Arrange the pineapple rings in a single layer in the pan, pressing them down into the hot syrup. Place a cherry in the center of each ring.

Cream the shortening in a large mixing bowl. Add the granulated sugar gradually, beating well. Add the vanilla and the eggs, and continue to beat until the mixture is well blended and light. Stir together the flour, baking powder, and salt in another bowl. Add to the creamed mixture along with the milk, beating for about 30 seconds, until the batter is smooth. Spread evenly and carefully over the pineapple rings, not disturbing their arrangement.

Bake for 35 to 40 minutes, until a skewer inserted in the center of the cake comes out clean and thick, syrupy juices are bubbling around the edges. Remove from the oven and let cool for 5 minutes. Place a serving plate upside down over the skillet, invert, and remove the skillet. Serve warm with whipped cream. ᴂ—

BLUE RIBBON GINGERBREAD

—◌ Gingerbread existed in medieval times, and it was given as a gift like a box of chocolates. The original gingerbreads always had honey as a sweetener, and if you want to honor the past, add 1 tablespoon of honey to the following recipe.

This Blue Ribbon recipe pays tribute to the old-fashioned gingerbread—dark and spicy. Serve warm with whipped cream or ice cream.

2½ cups all-purpose flour
1 teaspoon ground cinnamon
2 teaspoons ground ginger
1 teaspoon ground cloves
8 tablespoons (1 stick) butter, softened
½ cup sugar
1 cup dark molasses
1 tablespoon honey *(optional)*
2 teaspoons baking soda
1 cup boiling water
2 eggs, lightly beaten

Preheat the oven to 350 degrees. Grease and lightly flour an 8-inch square pan.

Sift the flour, cinnamon, ginger, and cloves together onto a piece of waxed paper.

Put the butter in a large mixing bowl and beat until it is smooth and creamy. Add the sugar and molasses (and honey, if you wish), and continue beating until well blended. Mix the baking soda and boiling water and pour into the butter-sugar mixture, beating well. Add the flour mixture and continue to beat until the batter is smooth, then beat in the eggs.

Pour the batter into the prepared pan and bake for 45 to 55 minutes, until a toothpick or broom straw inserted in the center of the cake comes out clean. Remove from the oven and let cool in the pan for 5 minutes, then turn out onto a rack. Serve warm. (Some like this gingerbread cool, so try it both ways.) ✑

VISIONS OF GINGERBREAD

I love gingerbread in its true cake form—moist, spongy and spicy. It is strictly home food, but no one makes it any more. Those who crave it get their fix from mixes, and if you give them the real thing, they appear confused. Why doesn't *their* gingerbread taste that good? There is nothing to be said about mixes: they are uniformly disgusting. Besides, gingerbread made from scratch takes very little time and gives back tenfold what you put into it. Baking gingerbread perfumes a house as nothing else. It is good eaten warm or cool, iced or plain. It improves with age, should you be lucky or restrained enough to keep any around.

—Laurie Colwin,
Home Cooking

BAKED ALASKA

—☙ The wonder of Baked Alaska: its frozen filling remains ice cold although it comes right from the hot oven. The secret of this true American dessert, invented by a physicist around 1800, is that the ice cream, resting on sponge cake, is covered by meringue, which is browned in the oven so quickly that the ice cream doesn't have time to melt. Any kind of ice cream that appeals to you can be used.

Lazy Daisy Cake *(page 196)*
4 egg whites
1/8 teaspoon cream of tartar
1/2 cup sugar
1 quart ice cream, frozen hard

Preheat the oven to 450 degrees.

Make the cake (but not the topping). Choose a board that will fit into your oven, wet it on both sides, and then shake off the excess water. Spread a piece of brown paper on top of the board and place the cooled cake on it. Put the egg whites and cream of tartar in a bowl and beat until foamy. Slowly add the sugar and continue to beat until the egg whites are stiff but not dry. Cut the ice cream in slices to cover the top of the cake, leaving a 1/2-inch rim of cake all around. Cover the ice cream and cake completely with the meringue. Lightly brown in the oven for about 5 minutes. Serve at once. ☙

CHILDREN'S
CHOCOLATE-CHIP SQUARES

⟶ Encourage children to learn to cook and bake when they're young. This is a simple recipe they'll love.

1½ cups all-purpose flour
1½ teaspoons baking powder
½ teaspoon salt
1 cup sugar
⅓ cup vegetable oil
2 eggs, lightly beaten
½ cup chopped nuts
2 cups (12 ounces) semisweet chocolate morsels

Preheat the oven to 350 degrees. Grease and lightly flour an 8-inch square pan.

Toss together the flour, baking powder, salt, and sugar. Add the vegetable oil and eggs, and beat until thoroughly combined (the mixture will be stiff). Stir in the nuts and chocolate morsels. Scrape the dough into the prepared pan and use your moistened fingertips to smooth the top and spread it evenly.

Bake for about 30 minutes, or until the top is golden brown and a toothpick inserted in the center comes out clean, or with just a residue of chocolate on it. Remove from the oven and let cool in the pan on a rack, then cut into 2-inch squares. ⟶

CARAMEL-COVERED STUFFED DATE ROLLS

—⌒ An all-time favorite: Each date is stuffed with a walnut half (or bits of walnut), dipped into the batter, baked, and then frosted. These keep very well and are marvelous for mailing and shipping.

60 pitted dates
60 walnut halves, or about 1 1/2 cups large walnut pieces
4 tablespoons (1/2 stick) butter, softened
3/4 cup packed light brown sugar
1 egg, lightly beaten
1/2 cup sour cream
1 1/4 cups all-purpose flour
1/4 teaspoon salt
1/4 teaspoon baking powder
1/2 teaspoon baking soda
Caramel Butter Glaze *(recipe follows)*

Preheat the oven to 400 degrees and get out some cookie sheets.

Stuff each date with a walnut half, or 2 or 3 walnut pieces, and set aside.

Beat the butter, then slowly add the sugar, continuing to beat until smooth and blended. Add the egg and beat well, then stir in the sour cream. Toss together the flour, salt, baking powder, and baking soda. Add to the butter-sugar mixture and beat just until smooth and blended.

This is the sticky part, but it's worth it: With your fingers, dip each of the stuffed dates into the batter and place it on the ungreased cookie sheet, leaving about 1 inch between cookies. The batter will not form a smooth coating over the dates; it will look patchy, but this is fine. Bake for 8 to 10 minutes, until lightly golden around the edges. Remove from the oven and transfer to racks. While the first batch bakes, prepare the glaze so you can spoon it over the cookies while they are still hot. ✑

CARAMEL BUTTER GLAZE

MAKES 1 CUP

6 tablespoons (¾ stick) butter
1½ cups confectioners' sugar
½ teaspoon vanilla
About ¼ cup cold water

Melt the butter in a small saucepan and continue to cook, swirling the pan by the handle, until the butter is lightly browned. Remove from the heat and stir in the confectioners' sugar, vanilla, and enough water to make a runny glaze. Continue to stir until smooth. Drizzle over the cookies with a teaspoon, or apply with a brush. ✑

THE LONELINESS OF THE FAST-FOOD EATER
(NOT ONLY IN AMERICA)

[Fat is] the outward and visible sign of a profound social disaster: the decline of the meal. We have to face this threat if we want to face it down.

Mealtimes are our oldest rituals. The companionable effects of eating together help to make us human. The little links which bind households together are forged at the table. The stability of our homes probably depends more on regular mealtimes than on sexual fidelity or filial piety. Now it is in danger. Food is being de-socialised. The demise of mealtimes means unstructured days and undisciplined appetites.

The loneliness of the fast-food eater is uncivilising. In microwave households, family life fragments. . . . Part of the result of the snacking society is undermined health, as eating disorders multiply. People alienated from the comradeship and discipline of the common table starve and stuff themselves into extremes of emaciation and obesity. . . .

So the family mealtime looks irretrievably dead. The future, however, usually turns out to be surprisingly like the past. We are in a blip, not a trend. Cooking will revive, because it is inseparable from humanity: a future without it is impossible. . . .

A return to the table is inevitable because, as Carlyle once said, "the soul is a kind of stomach, and spiritual communion an eating together." We seem incapable of socialising without food. Among people who like to enjoy others' company, every meal is a love feast. We eat to commune with our gods. The discreetly lit table is our favourite romantic rendezvous. At state banquets, diplomatic alliances are forged. Deals are done at business lunches. Family reunions still take place at mealtimes. Home is a place which smells of cooking. If we want relationships that work, we shall get back to eating together. Along the way, we shall conquer obesity: if we stop grazing, we shall stop gorging.

—Felipe Fernandez-Armesto,
The Guardian (London),
October 2, 2002

HERMITS

⸏∽ There are many recipes for this native New England cookie, all with varying amounts of spices, fruits, and nuts. Hermits originated in the days of clipper ships; because they kept so well, sailors used to pack them in sea chests and take them on their voyages. Give this recipe a try—you'll most certainly like it.

12 tablespoons butter (1¹/₂ sticks)
²/₃ cup granulated sugar
³/₄ cup packed dark brown sugar
2 eggs, lightly beaten
3 cups all-purpose flour
¹/₂ teaspoon salt
1 teaspoon baking powder
1 teaspoon cinnamon
1 teaspoon ground cloves
¹/₂ teaspoon ground ginger
¹/₄ cup dark molasses mixed with ¹/₈ cup warm water
1 cup golden raisins
1 cup chopped nuts

GLAZE

1 egg, well beaten

Preheat the oven to 350 degrees. Grease 2 cookie sheets.
Cream the butter with the sugars, then beat in the eggs. Toss the flour, salt, baking powder, cinnamon, cloves, and ginger together, then add to the butter-sugar mixture along with the molasses mixture. Fold in the raisins and nuts. Plop one-quarter of the batter onto a cookie sheet, and shape it with floured hands into a strip about 10 by 3 inches; repeat with another quarter of the batter, spaced several inches apart. Do the

same with the remaining batter on the second cookie sheet. Paint the tops of the 4 strips with egg glaze. Bake for 15 to 20 minutes, depending on how crisp you like your Hermits. While still warm, cut each strip into 9 bars. ᧞

The Heart of the Chef

If you don't love others, you can't cook. People who have no love to share eat poorly, and they don't cook. If you love cooking, you will cook, at whatever level. People who like to be around a table, who like to share—they'll try to cook, even if it's only an egg. I would much prefer to eat an egg with friends than caviar with strangers.

—Chef Philippe Legendre, formerly of Taillevent, quoted in Andrew Todhunter's forth-coming book (Knopf, 2004) about a meal at Taillevent

SCHRAFFT'S
BUTTERSCOTCH COOKIES

....

MAKES ABOUT 30 LARGE COOKIES

—⌒ This is a cookie with a past. My editor, Judith Jones, remembers fondly these big, rich, crisp cookies that she used to get as a child from the nearby Schrafft's. Schrafft's was originally a Boston company, but it had thriving bakeries and restaurants all over New York that have since disappeared. So we asked James Beard where we could get the original recipe. Judith wanted to include it in the book about New England she was writing with her husband, and I wanted it for my *Fannie Farmer Baking Book.* James, as always, responded in a flash and procured the recipe from the retired head of the company. The formula was for about 20 pounds of cookies and called for hydrogenated industrial products we'd never heard of. "Just use Crisco and a little butter," James advised, and so we did, reducing the amounts to workable numbers. The cookies are always a great hit with anyone tasting them for the first time, and will bring back memories for those who grew up on Schrafft's.

2 tablespoons butter, at room temperature
3/4 cup vegetable shortening, at room temperature
    (James Beard always preferred Crisco)
1¼ cups packed dark brown sugar
1 egg
2 tablespoons nonfat dry milk
1 tablespoon vanilla
1¾ cups all-purpose flour
½ teaspoon baking soda
½ teaspoon salt
1 cup finely chopped pecans

Preheat the oven to 375 degrees. Grease cookie sheets.

Combine the butter and shortening in a large mixing bowl and beat for a few seconds. Add the sugar and beat until creamy. Add the egg, dry milk, and vanilla and beat until light. Stir the flour, baking soda, and salt with a fork to mix and lighten. Add to the sugar-butter mixture and blend. Stir in the pecans and mix well.

Drop heaping tablespoonfuls of dough 2 inches apart onto the cookie sheets. Dip the bottom of a glass 3 inches in diameter into flour and use it to press the dough down in a circle of the same dimension. If the dough sticks a little as you lift off the glass, scrape it from the glass and just pat any bits back into the circle of dough to make it even and neatly round. Dip the glass into the flour again after each pressing.

Bake the cookies for 7 to 10 minutes, until golden brown. Remove from the oven and gently lift the cookies onto a rack. Let cool and store in an airtight container. ∽

CHOCOLATE ICEBOX COOKIES

—⁀ Once you have tasted a day-old cookie next to a freshly baked one just out of the oven, you will forever be spoiled by the dramatic difference. This recipe is a double winner; first it is chocolate, and second, it is fresh baked. I think that probably most cookie doughs can be refrigerated and then baked as needed, but I have never put this to a test.

1/2 cup vegetable shortening
2/3 cup sugar
1 egg
1 teaspoon vanilla
1 1/2 cups all-purpose flour
6 tablespoons unsweetened cocoa
1/2 teaspoon baking soda
1/4 teaspoon salt
1/2 cup shredded coconut

Cream the shortening and sugar together, then add the egg and vanilla and beat until light and fluffy. Put the flour, cocoa, baking soda, and salt into a sifter or strainer and sift them over the sugar mixture. Beat until the dough is completely blended and smooth. Stir in the coconut. Shape the dough into rolls about 1 1/2 inches in diameter, then wrap in waxed paper or plastic wrap and chill until firm (the dough will keep for several days in the refrigerator).

Preheat the oven to 350 degrees. Grease 2 cookie sheets.

With a sharp knife, slice the dough into 1/3-inch-thick rounds. Place them about 1 1/2 inches apart on the cookie sheets and bake for 8 to 10 minutes. Remove from the sheets and let the cookies cool on a rack.

DAINTY PRALINES

—❧ Because candy making at home has all but disappeared, along with butter churning and preserving, no one thinks of making pralines anymore. These slightly grainy brown sugar–pecan candies are so good, I wish I could get everyone to try to make them just once.

2¹/3 cups packed light brown sugar
1 cup heavy cream
¹/4 teaspoon salt
2 cups coarsely chopped pecans or walnuts

Put the sugar, cream, and salt in a 3-quart or larger heavy-bottomed saucepan. Cook over medium heat, stirring until the sugar has dissolved. It will now take 15 to 20 minutes to finish cooking. Let the syrup come to a boil, without stirring. It will boil up, becoming foamy with large bubbles, but it will soon settle down and the bubbles will become smaller and the foam will subside. Cook until the syrup reaches 238 degrees on a candy thermometer, or until it reaches the soft-ball stage. Start testing after 10 to 12 minutes.

I prefer the soft-ball test because it is easy and it doesn't require a thermometer. This is how it works: Have a small cup of cold water near the cooking syrup, and drop about ¹/2 teaspoonful of boiling syrup into the cold water. Gently roll the syrup between your fingers, and if it holds together in a soft ball, it is ready to remove from the heat.

Have a long piece of waxed paper spread on the counter. Remove the syrup from the heat and stir in the pecans; then stir briskly for about 1 minute. As soon as the syrup begins to look like it's getting firm, drop rounded tablespoons of it onto the waxed paper. Let cool completely, then remove from the paper and store in an airtight container between pieces of waxed paper. Or freeze. ❧

CANDIED GRAPEFRUIT PEEL

....

—ᒉ Home cooks of long ago wasted nothing in the kitchen that could be made edible. A triumph of their ingenuity was using grapefruit—or orange or lemon—peelings in a very simple fashion to make candied citrus peel, a wonderful treat anytime or anyplace. Candied citrus peel makes a great holiday gift. And a spoonful is always good on vanilla ice cream.

2 grapefruits *(see Note)*
2¹/2 cups sugar
³/4 cup water

Cut each grapefruit in half. Scoop out the pulp, leaving about one-eighth of the white pith with the peel. Save the pulp to have for breakfast or use cut up in a fruit salad. Cut each half grapefruit shell into ¹/4-inch-wide strips about 2 inches long. You should have about 3 cups of strips.

Put the grapefruit strips in a saucepan and add enough cold water to cover them. Use a plate that fits into the pan to cover the strips and keep them submerged in the water. Bring to a boil, remove from the heat, and drain off the water. Repeat this step 2 more times. After the third time, test a strip for doneness—a knife should pierce it easily.

Mix 1¹/2 cups of the sugar with the ³/4 cup water in another pan. Add the citrus strips and simmer until the peel becomes translucent and the sugar spins a thread—that is, when a little syrup scooped up in a spoon is poured off and forms a thread. To reach that point will take about 15 minutes of boiling, depending on your stove. When you can spin a thread, drain off the syrup and spread the citrus peel in a single layer on a rack or waxed paper to dry. Let it dry overnight, or for several hours.

Finish by tossing the citrus strips in the remaining 1 cup sugar. To preserve the peel, cover tightly in a jar. This will keep well for months, if you can keep from eating it all up right after it's made.

NOTE: To use orange and/or lemon peel, you'll need about 3 cups of strips. ⌒

.

INDEX

A NOTE ABOUT THE AUTHOR

Marion Cunningham was born in southern California and now lives in Walnut Creek. She was responsible for the complete revision of *The Fannie Farmer Cookbook* and is the author of *The Fannie Farmer Baking Book, The Breakfast Book, The Supper Book, Cooking with Children,* and *Learning to Cook with Marion Cunningham.* She travels frequently throughout the country giving cooking demonstrations, has contributed articles to *Bon Appétit, Food & Wine, Saveur,* and *Gourmet* magazines, and writes a column for the *San Francisco Chronicle.* In May 2003 she received the Lifetime Achievement Award of the James Beard Foundation.

A NOTE ON THE TYPE

This book was set in a modern adaptation of a type designed by the first William Caslon (1692–1766). The Caslon face, an artistic, easily read type, has enjoyed more than two centuries of popularity in our own country. It is of interest to note that the first copies of the Declaration of Independence and the first paper currency distributed to the citizens of the newborn nation were printed in this typeface.

Composed by North Market Street Graphics,
Lancaster, Pennsylvania
Printed and bound by Tien Wah Press, Malaysia
Designed by Virginia Tan and Carol Devine Carson